Worth a THOUSAND Words

Things I Want My Children to Know

Worth a THOUSAND Words

Things I Want My Children to Know

Cool Peaks Publishing
Denver, Colorado

Anthony Arvin
Volume I of the award-winning series

Worth a Thousand Words
Things I Want My Children to Know
Copyright © 2020 Anthony Arvin
All rights reserved.

No part of this book may be reproduced or distributed in any form
or by any means (written, electronic, mechanical, recording, photocopy or
otherwise) or stored in a database or retrieval system, without the prior written
permission of the publisher or author, except in the case
of brief quotations embodied in critical articles and reviews.

Books may be purchased in quantity and/or for special sales by contacting
the publisher or the author through his website: AnthonyArvin.com

Publisher: Cool Peaks Publishing
Cover and Layout Design, and eBook conversion:
Rebecca Finkel, F + P Graphic Design
Copy editing: Angela Thompson
Editing: Amanda S. Sorenson, Carpe Noumenon, LLC
Editing: John Maling, Editing By John
Publishing Consultant: Judith Briles, The Book Shepherd

Library of Congress Control Number: 2017950347
ISBN (soft cover) 978-1-945969-00-3
ISBN (hard cover) 978-1-945969-01-0
ISBN (e-book) 978-1-945969-02-7
ISBN (audio book) 978-1-945969-03-4

Publisher's Cataloging-In-Publication Data
(Prepared by The Donohue Group, Inc.)
Names: Arvin, Anthony, 1960–
Title: Worth a thousand words : things I want my children to know / Anthony Arvin.
Description: First edition. | [Denver, Colorado] : Cool Peaks Publishing, [2019]
Series: Things I want my children to know | Interest age level: Young adult.
Identifiers: ISBN 9781945969003 (softcover)
ISBN 9781945969010 (hardcover)
ISBN 9781945969027 (ebook)
Subjects: LCSH: Arvin, Anthony, 1960—Correspondence.
Conduct of life--Anecdotes. | Father and child—Anecdotes.
BISAC: FAMILY & RELATIONSHIPS / Parenting / Parent & Adult Child.
HUMOR / Form / Anecdotes & Quotations.
HUMOR / Topic / Men, Women & Relationships.
HUMOR / Topic / Marriage & Family. | LCGFT: Anecdotes.
Classification: LCC BJ1661 .A78 2019 (print)
LCC BJ1661 (ebook) | DDC 158.1/02—dc23

Family and Relationships | Marriage and Family | Anecdotes

First Edition
10   9   8   7   6   5   4   3   2   1
Printed In USA from 100% post-consumer (recycled) pixels.

To my wife, Belinda, who is my rock.
I could never be worthy of the sacrifices she has made,
and the devotion she has shown over these many years.

To my parents, and especially my dad,
with whom I shared an extraordinary bond.
It was he who taught me a passion for learning,
the toughness required to make it in life,
and the drive to seek wisdom.

Contents

Foreword 1
Author's Note 3

Four and Seven-Eighths 7
Porches 13
Of Cokes and Karma 17
Buffer Time 25
Beaters, Clunkers, and Junkers 29
Character 39
Giving a Horse His Head 47
Conditional Love 51
Uh-oh. What's Changed? 57
Crabs in a Basket 65
Getting Bitten 71
Cross Your T's 77
Seen but Not Heard 83
Even the French 89
I Am Merely a Guest There 97
Life Within Our Forts 107
Letting the Smoke Out 115

The Tool Shed 121
Reality Checks Don't Bounce 129
Reasonable Expectations 139
Yeah, Right! Opposites Fight! 145
The Art of Volunteering 153
I Can Live with That 159

Acknowledgments 173
Preview of Volume II:
What's Not to Trust? 175
About the Author 187
A Note from the Publisher 189
Working with the Author 190

Foreword

When I first discovered Anthony Arvin, I was excited by his captivating storytelling. His insights were profound, his delivery was entertaining and the nostalgia was simply mesmerizing. The collection of letters and stories that formed the basis for *Worth a Thousand Words* are easy to read and hard to put down.

To my delight and great surprise, a perfect revelation surfaced after we thought the book was finished. My team and I discovered Anthony's skill and background as an illustrator. His illustrations are stunning. The style and quality of Anthony's work remind me of the hours I spent marveling at Norman Rockwell's illustrations and looking forward to the weekly *Saturday Evening Post* when I was a kid. And, lucky for us, Anthony's wonderful drawings are now an integral part of each of the four volumes currently in production.

His wise words, coupled with his drawings, will leave you with a smile. It is my sincere desire that you enjoy the gift you are about to open.

I am honored to introduce you to Anthony Arvin.

—Judith Briles
The Book Shepherd

Author's Note

There is an old African proverb which claims, "When an old man dies, it's like burning down a library."

I consider this profound ... unless, of course, he was an idiot. Then, I imagine, it was more like someone set fire to the outhouse. Both were a loss, but for significantly different reasons. One was full of wisdom, and the other full of...well...you know.

This book is drawn from a collection of letters, porch stories and sometimes questionable conclusions that make up the library of my knowledge to date. They were written for my children, and their children, over nearly a quarter of a century. They are a little irreverent, a little sassy, and a lot salty. Except for the parts I made up, it is all true.

—Anthony Arvin

Love isn't a thing;

it is a process.

It is not just a feeling;

it is a state of mind.

To remain in that state requires

the building of a relationship—

one built on the unselfish desire

to fulfill the needs of the other.

Four and Seven-Eighths

The next few seconds were a blur, so I'm not certain what happened, but I feel fairly confident your mom clocked me with something.

I remember the night I got the call. One of your college buddies wanted to let me know that you were on your way to the hospital. He assured me it was nothing serious. He said, "Brandon just got a finger caught in a sprocket while working on the robot." When I asked how bad it was, I was told that your ring finger was "slightly amputated." I remember thinking ... slightly amputated? Isn't that like being sort of dead or partially pregnant? Isn't an amputation a specific condition?

You were in surprisingly good spirits when we got to the emergency room. The doctors had sewn it up but hadn't bandaged it yet, and that was okay with you. You said that you really wanted pictures. Then you said something about "chicks digging scars."

I still have those pictures, but other than your sister, I haven't had any girls take me up on the offer to see them. I think your sister's response was something along the line of, "It sucks to be you." I guess working on an ambulance jaded her. You'll have to do better than that if you want to impress her.

After seeing your hand, I did understand what "slightly amputated" meant, and it was a reasonably accurate description of the situation. Just losing the tip of your finger isn't really like having the whole thing amputated. You would be cosmetically altered, but it wouldn't be like losing the use of the finger.

I try really hard to be sensitive and caring and all that stuff, but sometimes I just can't help myself. While your mom was trying to find words to comfort and reassure you, I couldn't keep from pointing out that you'll never be able to "high five" anybody again. The best you can do is "four and seven-eighths."

The next few seconds were a blur, so I'm not certain what happened, but I feel fairly confident your mom clocked me with something—and maybe more than once. She denies it to this day, but the ringing in my ears and the stinging pain up the side of my head could lead me to no other conclusion.

But, you see, inside my still-twitching brain I was celebrating the fact that your injury wasn't considerably worse. You were only a blink away from losing four whole fingers. As it turns out, you were very fortunate, and for that, I was grateful. I also figured that since you weren't in a great deal of pain, you were doubly lucky. I felt it perfectly appropriate to ponder aloud *whether or not you would now have a limp when you type.*

Of course, I see the negatives, but I am convinced it really doesn't benefit anybody to dwell on them. If you sit around and think about those things, it will get you down, and overcoming adversity is hard enough without adding depression to the mix.

Over my lifetime I have learned the value of looking for humor in misfortune, and the peace that comes with counting your blessings, even in times of tragedy.

This was never better illustrated than when your granddad suffered his debilitating brain injury. Our Christmas dinner got cold on the dining room table while we all paced the floor in the intensive care waiting room—mortified by the prospect that this would be the day that everybody dreads. After months of surgeries, a coma, and rehab, Dad survived ... but with serious limitations. Second to your mom, Dad is my best friend, and we love doing things together. The brain injury left him extremely feeble, and those long conversations and brainstorming sessions that I treasured would be no more.

After seeing the severity of his injury, one of my friends exclaimed, "What an awful Christmas Day that must have been!" When she made that statement, though, it struck me that this could have been much worse. We could have lost him altogether. She was referring to the severity of his loss, but I was suddenly aware of what we got to keep.

Even though we will never again be able to carry on a conversation, I am thankful beyond words that Dad lived and still thrived. With him now in his seventies, and me in my fifties, I can sit for hours just holding his hand. He will pat my hand to assure me that he loves me. I don't have to assure him of anything; he can see it in my eyes. When I take him places, I still hold his hand—partially to help him walk, and partially just because I can.

Throughout your life—no matter what happens to you—never fail to count your blessings. It is rare that something so bad happens that you can't benefit by looking for the positive.

It is even more rare that you can't benefit from seeing the humor in a tough situation—even if the best you can do is respond to a "high five" with an enthusiastic "four and seven-eighths."

When you choose

to hold everyone

in high regard...

you will be amazed to see

how many other problems

in your life

just mysteriously

go away.

Porches

*In short, he surmised,
our decks are for showing off.
I agree. Decks
just aren't porches.*

In the movies, city people's front porches are magnificent affairs, designed to set the tone for the sophistication and refinement the visitor is certain to find inside. The entry will be a grandiose sight, surrounded by beautiful landscaping, large columns supporting an utterly useless roof, and an entry door that cost more than my first car. Likewise, Hollywood loves portraying the front porch of country people as the place where folks display their fine collection of surplus furniture littered with slack-jawed yokels sitting around in their bare feet, spitting tobacco and playing banjos. For country people, this is a really irritating stereotype. We always wore shoes when we sat on the porch.

An old country comedian, James Gregory, once had a routine where he bemoaned the fact that we have decks these days, not porches. We spend our time on the deck where we cook, entertain, and socialize. We decorate them with expensive furniture and lights and sometimes we even equip them with music. In short, he surmised, our decks are for showing off. I agree. Decks just aren't porches.

In the years before my grandparents were killed, they lived on a farm, and they had a wonderful porch. I loved it. It was a different era. The men worked in the fields all day while the women cooked, cleaned, canned food, and sewed the bulk of the clothes.

At the end of the day, the porch became the setting for the most special time of the day. It was a time for rocking, whittling, telling stories, reflecting on life, and passing knowledge from elder to youngster.

If you never had the experience of everybody congregating on the porch at the end of the day, take my word for it—time on the porch was different.

Typically, the men would arrive on the porch first while the women cleaned up from the evening meal. Often the men were still focused on work, so their discussions were work-related. By the time the women joined them, the men likely would have moved on to telling fishing stories or teasing us kids.

From time to time the discussions would branch off into two separate conversations—the men talking about one thing, the women another. But, the conversation would inevitably shift to politics, religion, gossip or family, and when that happened, both men and women would usually drift back into the same discussion.

While the adults talked, my brother and I would quietly play on the porch with our toy cars, trucks, and tractors. Sometimes we would lie in the cool grass and watch for falling stars. Air conditioning was rare on the Prairie in those days, so people would open up the windows and doors to let their house cool off before bedtime. All of those windows and doors were equipped with screens which collected all kinds of bugs that kept my brother and I entertained. For all of us, evening was our favorite time of day, and the porch was just a great place to be.

Many valuable discussions took place on that porch. A lot of time was spent openly questioning the wisdom of certain choices. Quandaries were weighed, and decisions were second-guessed. Morals, values, and wisdom were openly discussed and debated. Of course, it wasn't all serious. Occasional yarns were spun, and jokes were told. Bonds were constantly reaffirmed. Morals, values, and maturity were openly taught, and wisdom was ultimately passed down from grandparents to parents and to grandkids.

It really is a shame that we don't spend time on the porch anymore. As it happens now, our days end without reflection time—or time to pass on lessons learned the hard way. Even if you never live on a farm, or if your porch is a lot different from the one I remember, I really think that you should consider ending some of your days "on the porch" like we did on the farm. No TV or music, just time to talk, reflect, and bond with your children. It would do wonders for your relationships—even if it happens on a deck.

Of Cokes and Karma

I had done nothing deserving of such disrespect and began seriously contemplating saving Karma the trouble and sending a Hindu post-haste onto his next life.

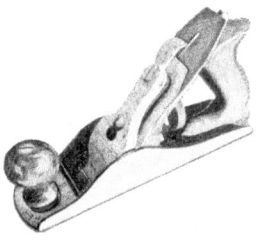

Many years ago, while working in India, I had gone several months without tasting anything that was even remotely familiar, so I was quite excited when I first discovered a Coca-Cola® for sale by a street vendor. At that time Cokes were strictly a black-market item in Bombay, but, to my surprise and delight, the beverage I wanted was prominently displayed within easy reach of this particular street vendor ... so I was ready to make a deal.

I made it clear what I wanted, the vendor quoted me a price, and I gave the scowling man my money.

He snarled as he put the money in the cash box, and then with all the contempt he could muster he reached right past the drink I just bought and selected a locally produced drink that cost one-tenth of what I just paid. Before I could object, he purposely opened it so that he couldn't take it back. When I rejected his offering, he threw it away in a dramatic fashion and then refused to give me the Coke, or my money back. At first, I was caught off guard ... followed shortly by getting really pissed. What had I done to deserve such rude treatment? I had done nothing deserving of such disrespect and began seriously contemplating saving Karma the trouble and sending a Hindu post-haste onto his next life.

I recognized later that this was a strange reaction because every once in a while I would lose money in a vending machine, but it didn't feel the same. Yes, losing the money was a little irritating, and it was a little disappointing having to go without the drink, but I was annoyed, not offended. Both ways I lost the money, and I still had no soft drink. Why did I experience such anger with a human but only felt annoyance with a machine?

The difference is disrespect. The human was disrespectful, and that is personal. For some strange reason, we tend to depend upon feedback from others to maintain our sense of value.

When a person shows us respect, we feel good and can easily respond with kindness. Conversely, when we are disrespected, we feel judged or criticized and we respond with anger or hurt.

Road rage is similar. If an animal runs into the street and we must slow down drastically, we may be annoyed, but not angry. If, however, another driver cuts us off and forces us to slam on the brakes, we feel disrespected and insulted.

When another motorist callously holds us back by driving slowly in the fast lane, or endangers our safety by tailgating, even when we are going as fast as the cars ahead of us will allow, that driver is indirectly communicating that we are not worthy of safety or the right of way. It's that apparent contempt, and that display of disrespect, that causes many people to experience road rage.

It's amazing (and a little frightening) to realize how much we depend upon this feedback—even from complete strangers—to affirm our value as a person. *When somebody shows us disrespect, it is as if we are getting kicked down the ladder to a lower caste.*

How, then, do you fix it? Several things come to mind. It helps to give people the benefit of the doubt. Don't assume that they were intentionally disrespectful. It doesn't happen very often, but I occasionally get preoccupied only to discover that I'm mucking up the flow of traffic. I don't go slow in the fast lane on purpose. But when I do, it is not because I am motivated by malice or condescension, and drivers who might make that assumption are absolutely getting it wrong.

There are certainly times when people experience genuine panic or crisis, and their aggressive driving has nothing to do with attempting to teach you a lesson, rather they are worried about getting to their destination as fast as possible. True, we know that those people we see driving insanely fast down the freeway are not speeding to the bedside of a dying loved one ... but if you give them the benefit of the doubt anyway, the stress just doesn't take over. Don't just forgive them; never indict them in the first place. Give them the benefit of the doubt.

The primary fix, however, comes from within you. So learn to assess your own worth and wean yourself from needing other people to affirm your value. Take stock of your own worth, based upon your value system, and stop expecting or even accepting the assessment of strangers. Don't give them power over you; save that for your Creator.

When you stop depending upon other people to affirm your value, you can be calm, cool, and collected—even when people are aggressively showing you disrespect.

I did, by the way, get my soft drink from my Indian vendor. You see, people in India take it seriously when visitors to their country get cheated. My vendor found himself with a whole face full of them ... and they were angry.

It seems that Karma didn't need my help after all.

Children learn
the same way adults do:
We gather a little information here,
a little there,
and then we fill in the gaps
with guesses.
Many times the problems
we struggle with in life
come from the guesses
we used to fill the gaps.

Buffer Time

Being on time to work can be as important to your career as your education, experience, and work ethic.

I didn't have a particularly good day. Having to fire someone is a miserable task. I hate it. I actually wonder if it isn't more painful to me than to the person being fired.

Most of our employees will be late only one or two times a year. The guy I had to fire accomplishes that by Wednesday of each week.

My parents' generation thought it was shameful to be late. They would rather be an hour early than a minute late. My generation was less paranoid about being prompt. We understood the importance of being on time for important things, but most of us didn't feel ashamed to be late for more trivial occasions.

I, for example, am not one of those people who don't want to be late just for the "principle." I make it to work on time because it is important to my employer. I don't, though, sweat being late for things that aren't important. I'm not going to beat myself up if I don't get to your uncle's backyard barbeque exactly on time. Same thing goes for the dentist who leaves me waiting in the lobby for nearly an hour regardless of when I arrive. On the other hand, I leave extra early when being late will cause me to suffer negative consequences, or when it will show disrespect for someone else. Now that you are entering the adult world, you will have to work this out for yourself.

When you venture out on your own, you must learn how to budget lots of things: money, time, and indulgences are three of the most significant. Being on time to work can be as important to your career as your education, experience, and work ethic. Failing to budget time was the downfall of the guy I had to fire. He was a great worker and a very nice guy, so I defended him for as long as I could. But being on time just wasn't important to him, so he didn't bother.

He would stay up late, get up late, and rush like mad trying to get to work. He figured out that it was only a twenty-minute drive to work, so he blew out the door at twenty 'til. What happened when traffic was bad?

He was late. What happened when traffic was bad three days in one week? He was late three times in one week. Each time he came dragging in late, he felt that he was the victim of circumstances beyond his control. He told me repeatedly that the delay was not his fault, and therefore we couldn't hold him responsible.

Sorry, but it doesn't work that way.

He was right about being the victim of circumstances, but he was wrong about those circumstances being beyond his control. When you don't allow time for a cushion, then you surrender control of your destiny to elements beyond your control (like traffic that backs up). But simply leaving earlier was all that was needed to regain that control. He didn't want to leave early. He didn't want to sacrifice any time for a cushion because it wasn't important to him to be prompt. As a result, he was a persistent victim of circumstances.

It is that simple. Buffer time is something you must build in if you are to be reliable.

Bad weather, needing gas, and slow traffic are all things you should be able to overcome and still make it to work on time. Buffer time is just part of the cost of being reliable. It is time you invest in keeping your job.

The earlier you head out the door, the better your chances of being on time. For occasions when it is critical that you arrive on time, such as when you are meeting a very important client at the airport, you budget even more buffer time. Buffer time gives you options for being rescued by a locksmith, tow truck, or even a taxi if necessary.

At most jobs, being on time is important. If you're habitually late, you will have to suffer the consequences. So, don't give "circumstances" control over your life. Leave early. Build in the buffer time. Control your own fate.

Beaters, Clunkers, and Junkers

We were just happy to have wheels because wheels meant freedom.

When I was in high school, most of the students who were lucky enough to own a car were able to inherit one from their family, or they worked a deal on something that had been previously driven by a neighbor. Now, let's get the cards on the table here. These weren't nice shiny cars with status, dignity, and paint. Most all of these cars had been ditched, propped on blocks, or left rusting in a field somewhere. Even though many of them were practically free, they still came at a great cost. In high school, pretty much everybody wants to be liked, and absolutely nobody could look cool in a 20-year-old station wagon. It was even worse if the engine smoked or if the car was adorned with rust spots in prominent places.

Many people affectionately referred to our cars as *jalopies* or *junkers*. The name *jalopy*, though, seemed to have an almost playful or cartoonish connotation so I tended to favor the terms *old beater* or *clunker*. Often, these vehicles bore little resemblance to the original make and model. Many had whole fenders or hoods of a completely different color. Others proudly wore a coat of primer that was just the first step of a grand plan to restore what we were just certain was going to be a classic.

These cars were so decrepit, or embarrassing, that even our parents—who were clueless about being cool—didn't want to be seen driving them. Whatever you chose to call them, one thing was for certain: *Beaters, clunkers,* and *junkers* were all notorious for guzzling gasoline, engine oil, and what little dignity the driver could feign.

Now, our little community was quite small, and most of the kids were in the same boat I was in. We were just happy to have wheels because wheels meant freedom. And, if all four of those wheels stayed attached for the entire trip, we considered ourselves blessed. I don't remember anybody in my school getting a brand-new car while we were in high school. However, we didn't live in a bubble, and we were exposed to the occasional teenager who did. Many came from the neighboring oilfield communities where they could afford really expensive new cars. One thing I can say quite emphatically: Many of my classmates and I swore we would never buy our own children a car while they were still in high school because so many of those kids were just horrible to us.

It wasn't enough that they would do their best to humiliate us because of our old cars, they smugly used their flashy rides as evidence that they were superior as human beings. We were relegated to a lower caste: the more embarrassing the car, the lower the caste. Cool ruled with a cruel and unforgiving sword.

Those cool kids were spared having to work all summer and pretty much every weekend after that, just to scrape together enough money for repair parts. They never missed hanging out with the fun kids because they were working on their cars. They never felt the sting of humiliation from having to drive an *old beater* that was so dilapidated it would often be mistaken for an abandoned vehicle—even, on occasion, while it was in motion.

The kids who drove new cars couldn't relate to the indignity we suffered at the hands of people who could not determine if our *old beater* was smoking as a normal indication that it was functioning, or if it was indeed on fire. Just so you know the difference ... if the smoke had a blue tint, the engine needed rings. If the smoke had a green tint and smelled sweet, the car needed new head gaskets. If, however, the smoke was nearly black or a bright white, then somebody needed to call the fire department. When you grow up in a community where most of the kids drive *old beaters,* you learn the art of interpreting smoke signals.

Looking back now, I can see that our embarrassing cars were the source of some really fond memories and more than a few funny stories. But, at the time, the humiliation that went with such vehicles just wasn't funny, unless, of course, it was somebody you didn't like who was doing the suffering. Humiliation is just part of growing up for most of us, and, during our school years, we tend to get abundant servings of humble pie. Our old cars provided an entire buffet of opportunities to be humiliated.

For many years I believed that the humiliation we suffered made us better people. I know that I developed a lot more empathy for people who could not afford nice things. Developing empathy was a good thing. Because I believed that developing humility made us better people, it only seemed logical that everyone should suffer the same shame we endured. That is why a lot of us vowed that we would never buy our kids a nice new car while they were in high school. In a nutshell, we didn't want our children to turn into the kind of cruel and hateful people who tormented us.

I no longer believe that we benefited from that kind of humiliation. Humility is something we should develop from within, not something that is forced on us by others. Humility can be desirable as long as it is the result of our own reflection and discovery. It is good when we recognize how small we really are in relation to the universe and how little we really understand in relation to the vast sum of human knowledge. It is even better when we come to realize our insignificance compared to that of our Creator. But that is different from humility that is the result of being embarrassed in front of our friends and classmates.

In an attempt to make your children better people, don't intentionally subject them to humiliation. It won't vaccinate them against being mean or harsh toward others, and the scars that come with this type of humiliation will often do damage that will last a lifetime.

I have also come to realize that the act of buying your children a new car won't make them into harsh and condescending people but raising them to believe they are somehow better than others likely will. If you honestly believe that some people are unworthy of respect, then your children will too.

The very embodiment of a caste system ... dividing people into groups according to their worthiness, begins to sort itself out along about junior high. Since we don't have caste systems based upon bloodlines or royalty, the kids begin to sort this out amongst themselves. In adolescence, kids instinctively begin trying to elevate themselves into a high caste by using ridicule and disdain to establish separation from those they deem as less worthy. The unworthy kids are kicked down the ladder to a lower caste, and then scorned so that they will remain there.

It is a cruel practice and one that some people never really grow out of. I know adults who, even as elderly people, are still very actively trying to keep the castes sorted out. They will specify those they consider to be worthy and those considered lacking. You have only to listen for their criticism—or praise. It's not difficult to determine how they have people sorted.

It is actually quite offensive, especially when loving and sweet people are seen as defective or undesirable just because they don't measure up to a standard considered important to the person being critical.

If you raise your children to believe that some people are worthy of high esteem, while others are not, for reasons as fickle as looks, money, race, or athletic ability, then your children are likely to grow up to be just as harsh as the kids who made us miserable. And, they are likely to miss out on some of life's greatest treasures ... some of the sweetest people alive, who were forced down to the lower rungs of society's ladder, and because of the humiliation they suffered, stayed there at the bottom, forever damaged.

When reality repeatedly bites you in the butt, faulty assumptions can usually be found lurking nearby.

Character

I had never seen such a vivid— yet very private— demonstration of character.

I started first grade in a southern Colorado mountain community on the Ute Indian Reservation. The economy wasn't great, and at some point my dad worked a second job at a gas station in town. In those days you didn't get out of the car to buy gasoline. An employee of the station filled your vehicle and then acted as cashier ... taking your money to the register and returning to your car with the change. Back then, nobody pumped his or her own gas.

One night, an elderly Ute Indian came to the gas station. He was broke, hungry, and needed gasoline. He wanted to trade a beat-up ranch rifle for a full tank of gas and enough cash for a meal. Dad couldn't stand to see anybody go hungry, so I imagine he would have given the guy what he needed without the trade. But as it happened, he traded his day's wages for the old man's very old rifle and four boxes of shells.

The gun really wasn't much to look at, and even less to shoot. The bullets were massive, and the gun smoked when you shot it. The slugs traveled so slowly you could hear them hit the target. In its day, it might have been quite a rifle, but after shooting it a few times, it appeared to have more use as a decoration. It would have looked really nice hanging over the fireplace in a rustic hunting lodge. But we didn't have a lodge.

As sometimes happens, though, the old rifle turned out to be quite a find. We found ourselves possessing an actual relic from the Old West—a genuine piece of history. The gun was manufactured in the mid to late 1800s and was a common saddle-gun during the days when the West was still very wild. Today that model of rifle is referred to as "The Gun That Won the West."

Considering its age, the rifle was in very good shape. Considering its history, the gun was enchanting. As you held it, you couldn't get away from the awe in realizing that this very weapon may well have been fired in the clashes between the Indians and Cavalry, or it may have been used to kill buffalo while the plains were still an untamed expanse. After all, we did get it from an elderly Ute Indian who was likely born while wagons were still crossing the Santa Fe Trail.

Suffice it to say, that old rifle was far and away our most prized worldly possession. Today one of those rifles in good condition sells for enough money to buy a new pickup truck. That rifle was the closest thing my dad had to a treasure. Everybody who visited our house was shown the gun. I remember it clearly.

Many years had passed before I realized that I hadn't seen the gun in a long time. When I asked, my dad told me he had given it to his older brother. I was shocked. At that particular time of his life, my dad hadn't been terribly close to his older brother. Why would Dad just give his most prized possession to his brother?

When I asked, my dad just bluntly stated, "It meant too much to me."

No more explanation was ever offered—or requested.

You see, he believed that it was wrong to place too much value on "things." God and family always came first, followed closely by the importance of integrity and honor. But at some point, he must have felt that something wasn't right. He must have determined that he was getting his priorities screwed up. As he went through the process of reassessing what he valued, he determined that the gun must go.

I had never seen such a vivid—yet very private—demonstration of character. If I had not asked, I never would have known. I doubt that Dad ever told another soul what he had done. Even my mom didn't know about it until she read this letter thirty-five years later. It was something that he did because he felt it needed doing—plain and simple.

It was a long time before I could really understand what he was trying to accomplish. When you get your priorities wrong, your life can spiral out of control. Possessions, aspirations, and status can be wonderful additions to your life, but when they become too important, you can find yourself living a life you don't want. Your possessions, desires—or even your ambitions—can end up owning you.

I hope you are never so poor that something as simple as an antique rifle could get your priorities all out-of-sorts. But you don't have to be poor to realize when the wrong things mean too much to you.

Be aware that ambitions, status, and the possessions that go with success can wreak havoc on your joy. When you find yourself losing sleep worrying about losing the things you own or the ground you have gained, you no longer own them. They own you.

It isn't just about possessions or money, either. The hectic lifestyles we tend to live today often amplify priority problems. Sure, you should enjoy your youth and your desire to squeeze every minute out of every day, but avoid letting activities become so important that they squeeze out the time that should be reserved for the things that are most important. If you find you don't have a spare minute, that your entire existence seems to be hurried, there is a pretty good chance that you need to stop and determine which things are adding to your life, and which are stealing your inner peace.

Decide what is important to you—your family, your faith, your values, whatever. Then keep those things where they belong, even if it means having to let go of some things you treasure.

Those who blindly believe

are passionate.

Those who actually understand

are confident.

It looks different.

Because it is.

Giving a Horse His Head

He explained that the packhorses had an easier time because they were given a long lead, and therefore did a better job of choosing their footing.

When I was young, backpacks were very crude and about as comfortable as carrying a picnic table piggyback. If that wasn't your idea of a good time, then a trip into the high-country wilderness meant riding horses. That was fine with me because horses were half of the fun. The only parts I didn't like were the rockslides.

Along the steep sides of deeply creviced canyons high in the Rocky Mountains, having to cross rockslides was pretty common and more than just a bit scary. The trail across a rockslide debris field can be nearly indistinguishable. There is no soil. You have to pick your way through a field of jumbled, jagged-edged boulders, some as large as refrigerators. Crossing on foot is bad enough, but crossing with a bunch of horses is downright scary. Falling would virtually assure serious, if not fatal, injury for either the horse or rider—or both. The old-timers assured my brother and me that we were safer on the horses than off, but that wasn't terribly comforting.

The horses were shod to protect their hooves from suffering cuts on the brutal terrain, but the metal shoes made the poor creatures slip and slide on the rocks. It was everything the animals could do just to stay on their feet. It was frightening to experience, especially from the back of a temperamental quarter horse that is struggling to keep its footing.

On one particular trip, while I was in my early teens, my dad noticed that my horse was having a lot of trouble on the rocks. As I emerged from a particularly scary rockslide, he motioned for me to look back at the packhorses that were still making their way across. He pointed out that even though each one of them carried a much heavier load than my horse, they had less trouble with the terrain. He explained that the packhorses had an easier time because they were given a long lead, and therefore did a better job of choosing their footing. He suggested that I loosen the reins so my horse could drop his head and study what he was doing. Then the horse could make it through with much less stumbling and slipping.

He referred to it as "giving a horse his head." Because of my fear, I was trying to fight the horse for control. As a result, I was making things more dangerous for the horse and myself. It takes a lot of trust and respect to surrender that kind of control to an animal, but as it turns out, doing so was good for both of us.

I learned that the wisdom of giving a horse his head isn't limited to horses on rocky terrain. Your mother and I spent the elementary years of your life helping you form your values, your direction, and your purpose in life. As you entered your teen years, we began to give you the freedom to make some choices for yourself. Sure, we stepped in when your safety was in jeopardy, but as you found your footing, we gave you more and more rein. When we did discuss your choices, we tried to discuss whether you were happy with your destination, rather than criticize how you got there. As it happened, you did very well.

The principle applies at work, too. Remember that those who are carrying the load often have the best perspective for getting you to your destination safely. As a manager, you need to surround yourself with people you can trust, then trust them. Respect them enough to give them the leeway they need to make decisions. If they occasionally stumble, give them the space they need to recover with their dignity intact.

Learning to loosen up a bit on the reins can be a very effective strategy that will serve you well at work and at home—even when you're on treacherous ground.

Conditional Love

Conditional love is intuitive; you will feel it naturally. Unconditional love isn't instinctive; it is a discipline.

Bless his heart ... even as a small puppy Jake wasn't bright, cute, or cuddly. He couldn't even play fetch. Jake was actually useless. If a thief had broken into our house, Jake would have been the first one on the scene—tail wagging, one ear up and one ear down, and that goofy "let's play" expression on his face. Still, he was somehow able to worm his way into our hearts.

When we first got Jake, we understood that some behaviors just come with new puppies. Puppies chew things. It's what puppies do. Puppies have accidents on the carpet. We knew that going in. It was a little disconcerting that Jake had so many accidents, but it didn't make us angry or force us to stop loving him.

When he chewed something up, we just chalked it up to having a puppy. When he made a mess, we just sighed and cleaned it up.

He did come with a few surprises. He shed a lot of hair. We still loved him. He had an insatiable appetite for attention. We loved him anyway.

Did we love Jake because he didn't have any faults? No. He had enough faults for several puppies. Did those quirks stop us from loving him? No. We loved him anyway. We knew what we were getting into, and our affection for him covered the tab. We were good with it.

Did we love him because of what he did for us? Absolutely not. He didn't actually do anything we needed done. His whole existence consisted of begging for our attention, sleeping, scattering his food, sneaking into the clothes basket (to shed hair on the clean clothes, of course), and antagonizing our older dog.

It could be argued that he didn't have any redeeming qualities outside of being totally nuts about us. He loved us unconditionally and adored the fact that we loved him. And by that one characteristic, Jake's tab was paid.

I learned a lot about unconditional love from Jake. When we forgot to feed him on time … he loved us anyway. When I failed to achieve a high status financially … it was not even on his radar. When we struggled in our relationships … he couldn't care less. He had no expectations that we perform. He never once removed his love from us ... even when we wouldn't let him have his way. We just couldn't keep from loving him back.

I think that when we marry, we should love our spouse the same way—unconditionally. Unconditional love willingly and freely grants the grace necessary to accept someone along with all of his or her imperfections.

I'm not talking about abuse; I'm talking about irritants. There are no perfect people; everybody is going to have irritating traits. If we love our spouse unconditionally, those irritating traits are gladly covered by grace, just as our love covered Jake's failings and as our faults are covered by our Creator.

Unconditional love extends beyond our spouse. When we have children, we need to do more than just love them unconditionally. We need to teach them how to love unconditionally, too. You can see very young children move from love to hate and from excitement to indifference, depending upon how they feel at the moment and depending upon whether or not you have told them "no" to something they want to do. Children instinctively exercise conditional love.

Conditional love is intuitive; you will feel it naturally. Unconditional love isn't instinctive; it is a discipline. It needs to be learned and practiced. It can be perfected only by regular reinforcement.

Unconditional love doesn't mean that you won't experience irritation from time to time, and it doesn't mean you should be a doormat either. It means that you work hard to hold the hard line without giving in to anger, and without judging harshly—even temporarily. To those you love unconditionally, you forgive and forget, even in the absence of an apology.

That is why even when you were irritating me, and I was pulling my hair out, you could always rest on the assurance that forgiveness was forthcoming, and apologies not required. (They would be nice, but not necessary.)

Part of learning to love unconditionally is learning to communicate that love, even when you would much rather lash out in anger. This can be really hard to do when somebody you love hurts you. It might take you a while to reflect on what has happened, and let go of the emotion, but do it. Make it work and move on.

You are human, so you will find yourself getting caught up in the emotion of the moment and reverting back to being critical or using anger to manipulate those you love. But when you find yourself slipping, learn to change course and get back on track. Keep working at it. Your goal is to never withdraw your love from your children, your spouse, or even just your puppy—even when you catch him sleeping on the clean laundry.

Rest in Peace, Jake.

Begin to look
for the good in people,
and begin
to elevate everyone.

Uh-oh. What's Changed?

... men will generally not remember a woman's outfit unless she does something radically different.

I know, my dear daughter ... it is a cruel reality that the kind, loving, and considerate man you married still hasn't noticed your new haircut, or that you've lost five pounds, or ... fill-in-the-blank. No, it isn't because he doesn't love you anymore, nor is it because he just doesn't care. It's because most men don't see the world through the same lens you do. You are not alone, and this is not a new problem.

Back in the 1960s, my grandmother claimed that she wore the same dress every day for a month, and my grandfather never once noticed. I can relate—with him. As a man, one of the phrases I dread most is: "Did you notice anything different?"

Now, I'm not an authority on how all men see women, but I think men tend to see the opposite sex the same way I do. Most of the time I don't even notice details like hairstyles and shoes. With the exception of sexually enticing clothing, men will generally not remember a woman's outfit unless she does something radically different.

Why don't we notice? I think we tend to sum up a woman as a whole package. We form an opinion based upon her overall appeal or "persona." The clothes, personality, disposition, style, charm, and attitude all play a role in the persona.

Narcissistic and delusional young men crassly rate a woman's looks on a scale of 1-10, but in the world of grown men, a woman's looks don't dictate her appeal. Sure, being attractive physically helps, but how appealing a person is depends upon a lot of things. A woman can have a movie star's good looks, but if she is mean I won't find her attractive. Conversely, a woman can be so appealing that I can't actually tell if she is physically attractive or not ... because her whole persona is absolutely beautiful and that overshadows my ability to assign value to her physical appearance.

Seeing a person through the lens of her persona can be a wonderful thing, but it also has its drawbacks, and the inability to *notice things* is one of those drawbacks.

I think the reason men don't notice haircuts or new dresses is that once a persona is established, we don't tend to dwell on the details.

Men don't find haircuts cute; we find women cute. If a cute woman gets a new haircut, we might really like how she looks, but we can't necessarily put our finger on what has changed. We are enthralled by her presence, not her accessories. We don't watch for details; we tend to enjoy and appreciate (or not) the whole persona. Only when I see a conflict in a woman's persona, will I sit up and try to take stock of what has changed.

To illustrate, picture in your mind the Hollywood-style stereotype of a librarian. She wears her hair up in a bun, has those tiny little wire-rim glasses suspended by a dainty little chain over a conservative, button-up sweater. She shushes you if you get too loud. That librarian could wear the same pastel-colored sweater every day for a year and men won't likely notice. She could change to a different color sweater and the men still won't notice. She might even change her glasses or hair color. It won't matter. As long as she keeps within her well-established persona, the details will be lost to most of the men she encounters.

Let her, though, show up at the pizza parlor with her hair in a ponytail, wearing a football jersey and some shapely blue jeans, and most guys won't even recognize her. She will look familiar, but they won't be able to put their finger on just who she is. Once she steps outside of the framework of the aforementioned persona, it is as if people are seeing her for the first time. In a way, they are. And right away the new persona begins to take shape, and she will start all over, just with a different persona.

It is interesting to note that this isn't just a *guy* thing. Women do it, too. The comedian Rita Rudner likes to taunt her audience with, *"Ask me what kind of car I drive,"* to which she gleefully responds, *"A white one."* Because of this, I can sort-of comprehend how it feels to be on the other end of the interaction. "What do you mean a *white* car? Is it a sports car? What kind of engine?" To a lot of women, the car might even have a persona. It is cute, or practical, or fun, but most of the women I know couldn't care less whether or not the car has an overhead cam under the hood. Nor are they likely to care what metal was used to make the rims. They are happy taking the car and assigning it a persona ... and it may as well be a pet. And when it comes to her pet, she sees its overall appeal, and the details just don't matter so much.

So, my daughter, stop worrying that he doesn't love you any more or that he doesn't care as much as before. Because it isn't about that at all. It is all about the different way that we are constructed. You can keep holding out hope that your husband will notice your new shoes or your new haircut ... but it is what it is. Your girlfriends and your mom are likely to be the only ones who will notice.

The remedy for negativity isn't positivity; it's gratitude.

Crabs in a Basket

If you have the drive to master your craft, and the tenacity to stay with it, you can be successful far beyond the limitations that others would force on you.

While I was working in India, I went with a friend to visit a fishing village on the shores of the Arabian Sea. As we walked along the rows of boats all unloading their catch for the day, he told me that many of the fishermen sell their catch—out of open baskets—right there by their boats. He also pointed out that a crab left in a basket by itself would climb out. However, by filling the basket with crabs, the fisherman trusts that all the crabs remain in place. Why? If any single crab were to try to climb out, the other crabs would grab ahold and pull it back down.

I grew up around rattlesnakes, not crabs, so I don't know whether this is fact or fable. The story, however, illustrates something you can expect to experience in your own life: If you dare to climb out of your basket, people around you will instinctively try to pull you back down. It is as if some people feel a moral obligation to "bring you down to earth." In this regard, "down to earth" means you shouldn't aspire to be more than *they* think you are worth.

Family and friends may be there for you when you have a tragedy, but surprisingly enough they can be very unsupportive and critical when they think you are striving for more than they think you should. You will sometimes find that those you expect to back you are actually judgmental and critical. They will sometimes even recruit people to ridicule you.

Most of my life I have had to strive for success in spite of people—sometimes even close friends and family. So listen closely when I say that you shouldn't succumb to their criticism. You can do anything you put your mind to. *If you have the drive to master your craft, and the tenacity to stay with it, you can be successful far beyond the limitations that others would force on you.* You can become a world-renowned chemist or a best-selling author. That is really up to you.

Family members who are not living out their dreams are possibly the worst about trying to force you into becoming the person they think you should be. Some will subject you to harsh criticism. Others will show mock support while they look forward to your failure.

But, they are not living out their dreams. Don't bow to their criticisms.

At one point or another, most everyone dreams of hitting that big-league home run. There is nothing wrong with going to bat with the full intention of hitting one out of the ballpark. There is nothing wrong with branching out and taking risks. Even your detractors may dream of what could have been, but they fear the humiliation that goes with big-league strikeouts. Maybe those who care for you want to spare you the humiliation that goes with strikeouts. Who knows why they do it, but my advice to you is to tune out the critics. Sure, listen to their reasoning, take it into consideration, but don't let their negativity scare you away from your dreams.

Don't fear the strikeout, and don't fear the failures. Until you get practice, you can't hit home runs. If you are too afraid to try, you never will.

Don't argue about it, and don't brag about your intentions. You don't have to be cocky or confrontational, just do it. Devise a plan, count the cost, and devote whatever resources are necessary to be successful.

You can't expect to succeed if you don't take the first steps. Make the sacrifices. Pay the dues and work to make good choices. If you do that, you are well on your way to success. But before you start, remember that people can be a lot like those crabs. Don't let the crabs pull you back down.

Those who suffer most from criticism are often quietly —but intensely— critical of others. When you see others through harshly critical eyes, you expect that everyone else is judging you in kind.

Getting Bitten

The poor thing was instinctively biting what it perceived to be causing its pain: me.

When an animal is injured in traffic, your first inclination is to help. You may even feel the urge to scoop the injured animal up in your arms and whisk it off to a vet. A surprising thing happens though; it will bite the fire out of you. Not just once either—it will bite you repeatedly until you let go. An animal does not comprehend your attempt to help. The animal only knows that it is in great pain and you are just making it worse. It probably doesn't help that, in nature, an injured animal becomes something else's lunch.

I've seen this firsthand. I once helped a friend transport her injured Doberman to the vet. It had a ruptured disc in its lower back and taking it to the vet caused great trauma for the animal. Just picking the poor thing up increased its pain tenfold. As a result, the minute I would get the poor yelping creature cradled in my arms, it would begin to bite me like I was a chew toy. The poor thing was instinctively biting what it perceived to be causing its pain: me. I noticed something interesting though; the bites didn't hurt so badly, and I didn't get angry.

If this dog had bitten me under different circumstances, it would have been a declaration of war. But under these circumstances the dog's suffering was my greatest pain, and the bites were nominal in comparison. Yes, we were both in a lot of pain, but this wasn't about me; it was about the intense pain the dog was feeling.

You can apply the same principle to people. *Next time your boss calls you into his or her office and wants to chew on you, try to focus on your boss's pain: not yours.*

It really works. Your boss can rant and rave, make threats and give mandates, followed then by blaming everything on you ... even when it isn't your fault. My natural reaction to being attacked (verbally) is to defend myself. I look for opportune times to try and defend my actions or decisions. It becomes a game of "who's guilty" as opposed to "how can we fix this."

If, however, you can let your boss chew on you while you are focusing on what is wrong (trying to determine what is causing the pain), you can shift it toward a conversation where you are looking for a solution to help him or her get rid of the pain. You can take a very negative situation and turn it into a good thing. You can become the hero instead of the heel. It really does work.

It also works for people who answer to you. When people you supervise come to you upset, set your ego and feelings aside so you can pay attention to them and focus on the pain that is driving them.

I understand that sometimes people will get frustrated with me. I can get wrapped up in the pressure and stress of the moment and be demanding and insensitive. The problem is made worse because many of your best employees won't tell the boss what he or she is doing that is making their life miserable, at least not until they are so emotionally invested that it results in a blow-up. Despite having a large and imposing stature, I usually don't get upset when people take me to task. Shooting the messenger doesn't help solve the problems that caused the anger in the first place.

Although I gently remind them to remain respectful, I absolutely allow employees to get upset and vent to me—even when it is about me. I will let them vent, and I will listen to their grievances. And specifically, I'll listen for signs of what is causing the pain so we can fix it. I am free to creatively explore a solution without having to worry about being right or pushing back to protect my ego.

This also works with your spouse. When you get to the point where you are always defending yourself in arguments, it may be a sign that you are focusing on your own pain, instead of the pain your spouse is experiencing. When you find yourself having the same argument over and over again, it is a sure sign that your spouse is feeling a pain that you are not understanding.

When we learn to listen for the pain others are feeling, we can find ourselves fighting less and understanding more, which is especially important with loved ones. It really is one of the most powerful skills that you can develop to improve your people skills at work and to keep love alive at home.

Assumptions are cunning little buggers. They love to dress up, to appear credible, then go out and parade around as facts.

Cross Your T's

> *In the desolate expanses of New Mexico, there are a lot of places you don't want to get stranded.*

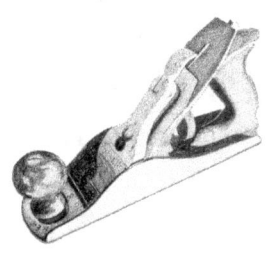

I have rediscovered something I never thought possible: I have again found my love for working on cars.

My first car was a Volkswagen Beetle, and I hated that car. Many years before I was old enough to drive, my dad grew tired of trying to keep it running and just left it parked. He, too, hated that car. When I turned 16, he offered it to me *for free* with the understanding that I was solely responsible for getting it running and keeping it that way.

Initially, the offer sounded like a great deal. History, though, repeated itself and the sweetness of the deal turned a little more sour each time the thing broke down. In the desolate expanses of New Mexico, there are a lot of places you don't want to get stranded. That car made certain I didn't miss any of them.

Have I mentioned that I hated that car? It ran flawlessly until I was in the middle of nowhere, during the heat of the day, then it would die. I got so tired of hitchhiking home that I finally bought something else.

For several years I tried to sell the car, but after failing to find a buyer, I took it to a VW dealership to see what I could get for it. The paint and body were flawless, so it should have been worth something. The car ran just fine all the way to the dealership. Of course, once I got there, it coughed, sputtered, backfired, and sounded like it was possessed by an unholy spirit. I paid more for the fuel in the gas tank than I was offered for the car.

Insulted and angry, I managed to coax the crippled car out of the parking lot and headed home. Just as we got out of sight of the dealership, it started hitting on all cylinders—never ran better. I'm pretty certain that car hated me, too.

Many months later, I decided to tune up the car one last time before trying—again—to sell the thing. I had replaced the plugs and points several times before, but the head of the screw that held the condenser was stripped, so I had never replaced the condenser. As it turned out, that oversight was unfortunate. This time

I took the time to remove the stripped screw. As I removed the condenser, its wire literally fell out. I wondered at the time if that faulty wire hadn't been the source of a lot of my grief.

I sold the car a week later. I nearly gave it away because I knew the guy and I didn't want him coming after me once he discovered its demonic disposition. Funny thing ... he drove that Volkswagen for years and it never once stranded him. I still hate that car.

Eventually, poor reliability made me hate working on any of my cars. I was good at figuring out what was wrong, but things wouldn't stay fixed. Over the past twenty years, though, that has slowly changed. For one thing, I now buy only high-quality parts. That reduces a lot of problems. I also take as much time as necessary, and I don't expect things to be easy. But those weren't the keys to solving my reliability problems. Reliability didn't come until I changed my attention to detail. I wasn't crossing my t's and dotting my i's.

That stripped screw cost me thousands of dollars in the sale price and who knows how much on replacement parts and towing charges over the previous years. The car wasn't the problem; I was the problem. The problem wasn't my ability; it was my discipline. I was into shortcuts. I took the path of least resistance.

With age I realize that the same principle applies to nearly everything we do. It doesn't matter if you are working on your car or writing a computer program. Deal with the details—all of them—not just the convenient ones. Deal with all of them. Develop the discipline to deal with the details, and you will find that your frustration levels fall, and your success levels rise.

I have no doubt that today I could make that stupid car a joy to own. But ... don't get me wrong ... I don't want it back.

An old adage says that "Still waters run deep." But I've also noticed that —on occasion— "Still waters smell like a swamp." Sometimes the hamster just can't figure out the wheel.

Seen but Not Heard

Your mom and I grew up in an era where children were expected to be seen but not heard.

I once read that our little spitfire, *Rockie Dog,* isn't unusual. The article explained that miniature dachshunds are, by nature, little emperors. Shyness in the breed is considered a fault.

Nothing could be more ironic because he is just so darned cute. If his legs were any shorter, he wouldn't be able to reach the ground. He just reeks of cute. But, that goes to show how misleading looks can be because Rockie Dog is a little tyrant.

Were he a little smarter, you might conclude that he resents being cute, and tries to make up for it by bullying everybody and everything in sight. It doesn't matter that he would be little more than an hors-d'oeuvre to the bigger dogs; he rules them without fear and without mercy. I personally think he resents being named after a ballpark frankfurter.

This is new to us. While we have had plenty of alpha dogs before, those dogs have always understood where they fit in the grand scheme of things. They learned to have an awareness of our space. They wouldn't step on us if we stretched out on the floor in front of the TV. They wouldn't pull lamps or cell phones off the end tables in the living room just because they couldn't be bothered with walking around the cords. They yielded when they observed that they were blocking the pathway.

Rockie Dog doesn't have any such awareness. He is the center of the universe. Everything and everywhere is his space. His interests and desires are his sole consideration when deciding where to go, or what to do. He is no doubt a tyrant, but he is so small and so cute that we let him get away with it.

Fortunately, for the rest of mankind, Rockie is confined to our house and yard. His influence over other people of the world is limited by his lack of mobility. Children, however, are not confined to the house. When children do not respect the space and rights of others, they too can become little tyrants. Unlike their canine counterparts, miniature human tyrants are not cute. When children have a blatant disregard for others, they spread misery everywhere they go.

Your mom and I grew up in an era where children were expected to be seen but not heard. When the adults were engaged in a conversation, we (children) weren't allowed to speak unless we were spoken to. It's a big country, so that tradition may still exist in some regions, but where we live now, that notion is as old-fashioned as canning your own vegetables.

We did expect you to be respectful of the adults and not butt-in or be rude, but you were absolutely allowed to speak up when you had something to say. As long as you were aware of your surroundings and were respectful to the inhabitants, we included you in conversations where children had not previously been welcomed.

On the flip side, we have all seen parents who don't teach their kids how to respectfully engage an adult in conversation and who can't even have the shortest of conversations without their children interrupting and badgering them. That doesn't benefit anybody—the parent, their guests, or the children. We have all seen children who have no sense of what is important to anyone else and don't care what is important to anybody else.

When children fail to respect the rights and feelings of everyone else, they have no problem making everybody in the vicinity miserable until they get their way. That isn't healthy.

Children who are raised without any sense of anyone else's needs may well be worse off than those who were stifled. When you raise your own children, the best thing you can do is to find a happy medium. Allow your children to feel important and to speak up. But don't allow them to develop the Rockie Dog syndrome. Children shouldn't be little emperors.

In our youth,

we placed faith in the words

of those we respected.

With experience, we learned

to judge people more

by their actions.

But, as you gain wisdom,

you learn to see the inevitability

of people's patterns.

Even the French

New Year's resolutions usually fail because we try to change ourselves by correcting behaviors, habits, and attitudes ... not our nature.

It might be easier to build empires than to make deep personal change.

Very few people ever make dramatic personal changes in their lives. I'm not referring to behavioral changes such as quitting smoking or losing excess weight—even though those are good things. And I'm not referring to major changes in relationships, careers, religion, or philosophies.

I'm talking about the kind of change needed to become the person you know you should be, the person your spouse needs and deserves, and the person your children need. Although I have gone through many changes in life, I haven't had much luck making such positive, personal changes stick. Despite my best efforts to change myself by correcting my behaviors, habits, and attitudes, I always reverted to my old ways because my nature remained the same. New Year's resolutions usually fail because we try to change ourselves by correcting behaviors, habits, and attitudes ... not our nature.

If you are selfish by nature, you cannot become unselfish without first changing your basic nature. Yes, you can mask your selfishness by forcing yourself to engage in unselfish actions. But acting out unselfish behaviors doesn't make you unselfish; it merely makes you an actor—an actor who is playing a role that contradicts your nature.

Trying to change yourself by acting differently is about as effective as trying to get rid of dandelions in the yard by picking the leaves. Some self-help books will give you tips on the best time to pick the offending leaves. Others will sell you tools for making short work of the leaves. Still, others will teach you how to happily coexist with the weeds. But the problem with dandelions isn't just the existence of the leaves; it is the existence of the whole weed. When you eliminate the root of the dandelion, the leaves don't grow back.

The good news is that getting to the root of the problem, and changing our nature, can be nearly painless. For me, all I experienced was a change of paradigm. One day I came to realize that most of our issues all come from the same basic cause, and that cause is created by a basic perspective that most all of us share. That perspective has to do with the way we see other people. The greatest change you can make—the one that helped me eliminate the majority of problems with my nature—required only that I change the way I view other people.

You see, the French aren't the only people who make arrogance a national pastime, although they do seem to excel in that endeavor. We are all subject to a little arrogance. It is a natural byproduct of our need for self-esteem. Arrogance may be more apparent in some than in others, like the French, but trust me when I tell you that most of us have it. We may not see it in ourselves, but arrogance causes a lion's share of the problems in our nature.

Look around at people you think could benefit from some serious change in their life, and then notice what they all have in common. Most of the time you will see that they have a high opinion of themselves and a low opinion of others. Those who suffer most from criticism are often quietly—but intensely—

critical of others. When you see others through harshly critical eyes, you expect that everyone else is judging you in kind. It is a bit difficult to believe that merely having a low opinion of others can be the root to so many of the problems in our lives. It isn't intuitive or obvious, but it is real. *Deciding to hold others in high regard is one of the secrets of maturing and being able to be at peace with yourself and everyone else.*

Because it is counterintuitive, changing your attitude toward others doesn't make a lot of sense. However, if you will commit to seeing the value in others, rather than pigeonhole them into a lower caste because of their faults, it will change you in a good and profound way.

The solution seems overly simplistic, but that is the beauty of it all. It only requires that we decide to respect and value everyone. Don't respect only the people you feel deserve it. Don't respect only the smart, the kind, the successful, the beautiful, or those who share your values. Respect everyone. Why? Respect them because it is good for you. Respect them to correct a fault in your nature ... a fault that poisons your relationships, attitudes, and sometimes even your health.

If you are struggling in your marriage, your job, or whatever, evaluate your attitude toward others. Make up your mind to respect everyone ... even the slow waiter, the surly little neighbor kid who talked your child into chunking rocks at the neighbor's greenhouse, and even those people who fail to respect you back. When you choose to hold everyone in high regard—even the French—you will be amazed to see how many other problems in your life just mysteriously go away.

I would much rather you be compassionate than caring. Caring is an emotion ... one that is often self-serving. It is trendy to say you care, but then settle for the gratification of being a good person without actually doing anything to improve the situation for those you claim to "care" about.

I Am Merely a Guest There

For years your mom has wondered out loud how I can walk by a full trash can and not notice that it needs to be emptied.

At one point in the second *Jurassic Park* movie, one of the scientists came to the unsettling realization that they had expanded the perceived territory of a Tyrannosaurus Rex. As a result, they were in deep trouble because this very angry creature would now feel the need to defend this "newly expanded" territory, and the scientists were stranded there. That was bad news for them, but it is good news for us, because it explains an age-old problem that couples face every day: the existence of our perceived territories and our need to defend them.

Your mom never ceases to be amazed that I want to be noticed for helping around the house. For thirty years she has thanklessly, endlessly, and pretty much anonymously done everything required to keep the household running. As a result, she looks at me like I just grew a third eye when I want a pat on the back for washing a load of jeans.

Why does it matter so much to me that she knows I am contributing? Despite any evidence offered by my in-laws, I wholeheartedly dispute that it is brain damage. Thankfully, the dinosaur illustration makes it easier to explain: We each have our perceived domains, and we do not compete for who is in control within those specific areas.

I think that in most homes, men are little more than guests. Offhand, the men I know instinctively view the house as the wife's domain. That probably explains why they don't feel responsible for its day-to-day operations. The wife wants control over what happens in the house. It is her domain.

Think about it. If I showed up with a new couch for the living room without including your mom on the decision, she would be miffed. It's her domain. When, out of the blue, she shows up with a new entertainment center, I am expected to be thankful and appreciative. Her domain. If I walked into the room where she is doing laundry and told her she is not using the correct detergent, she would look at me like I just climbed out of a spaceship. Her domain.

Still don't believe me? Imagine for a moment that I were to take apart something greasy right in the middle of the living room floor. In my shop, I can take something apart and leave it there until I decide to move it. Your mom couldn't care less. That is my domain. The living room is not. Any room in which she is perfectly comfortable haranguing me for making a mess is not my domain. I am merely a guest there.

If I don't load the dishwasher correctly? Her domain. If I don't dry the clothes on the correct setting? Her domain. If I have the wrong pan for cooking something? You get the idea.

It is further illustrated by putting the shoe on the other foot. Imagine that she went out into the woodshop when I wasn't around (my domain) and swept the floor and emptied all the trash. Now, do you think she wouldn't be expecting me to at least notice and to thank her? I have news for you. If she cleaned my shop and I failed to notice and thank her profusely, it would never happen again. The reality is, she would be just like me when I occasionally make the bed. She would expect me to notice and to express my appreciation that she went above and beyond her responsibility and did something for me in my domain.

An understanding of domain also explains another conundrum. For years your mom has wondered out loud how I can walk by a full trash can and not notice that it needs to be emptied. Yeah, yeah ... again with the brain damage. If she points it out to me, I am happy to deal with it, but unless she says something, I don't even notice. Not my domain.

In my defense, though, both genders do it. Imagine yourself going into a bathroom at a sports stadium. After you wash your hands, you go to discard the paper towels, but the trash can is overflowing. Do you think, "Hmmm ... I should empty that!" Of course not. You don't think you personally need to empty the trash can because it isn't your domain. You are simply a visitor. You don't control anything, and have no say in how things are handled, so you feel no responsibility for what needs to be done.

That is exactly how I feel in your mom's domain. I don't purposely shun emptying the trash. It simply doesn't occur to me because it is not on my radar. I am a visitor in the kitchen. I have no control and feel no responsibility. It is not natural for me to notice things outside of my domain.

If we were to agree that the kitchen trash becomes my domain, then everything changes. If it becomes my domain, I take ownership of it. It will be on my radar, and I will be free to do it how and when I want. It's my domain. I might buy a different trash can or switch to a different kind of trash bag. My domain. I might want to take it out when it is only ¾ full—or maybe my style will be to overfill it and smash everything down until it is difficult to empty. It's my domain. But if I am not free to do it my way, then it still isn't my domain, and I won't own it. I won't feel responsible.

Once you understand the concept of perceived domains, you and your spouse can use it to your advantage instead of endlessly ridiculing or resenting each other when things don't go as expected.

A good illustration of this came from a friend who told me about the strange way her husband washes dishes. He fills the whole sink with soapy water and washes everything. Then, instead of taking the clean dishes out as they are done and rinsing them with running water, he leaves all the soapy dishes in the sink while he drains the wash water and refills the sink with rinse water. He does this again and again until the rinse water is clear.

I must admit, I had never heard of anyone doing dishes that way. My friend went on to explain that when they were newlyweds, her mother warned her to not say a word about her husband's odd way of washing dishes. My friend's mom wisely explained that he should be left alone to do the dishes as he pleased, lest she end up washing the dishes herself. Thirty years later, he was still washing the dishes every day.

It is a credit to my friend and her mother for being wise enough to understand how this worked and let it play out. She gladly let her husband have dominion over the dirty dishes. He was the boss, he did it his way, and he owned it.

Upon hearing this story, one of her coworkers blurted out, "That is stupid. If he were my husband, I'd tell him how it should be done." We asked her, though, and sure enough, that coworker's husband never washed the dishes. She would never relinquish control, and he was happy to let her keep it. It's just a hunch, but I'm betting he never helps with the laundry or making the bed either.

Understanding whose territory you're in doesn't mean that you won't still have issues. There will be some tasks neither of you want to own. In other areas, you both want dominion and you will have conflicts over control. You will have to be mature enough to work through those issues. But for all other areas, especially as they relate to tasks around the house, recognizing the concept of letting each have his or her own domain will make it easier to cooperate and not leave one or the other with an unfair share of the load.

Then, maybe, she will quit pondering aloud whether you ate too many paint chips as a child, because—yet again—you left the vacuum out ... just so she'll notice that you've vacuumed.

It is amazing how

an electric train set

erases the half-century

between my grandsons and me.

When that train is

chugging around the track,

we are momentarily the same age

and filled with the same wonder.

Life Within Our Forts

Some people like to describe this act of creating a public persona as making masks to hide behind, while others like to describe it as building walls.

I love to observe Head Start and preschool children for a whole slew of reasons, not the least of which is having no awareness of how they look. A four year old who is perfectly calm and content one second can yield to the sudden compulsion to dance the funky monkey. Then, without compunction, settle back into the crowd as if nothing happened. The great thing is that none of the other children think anything strange went down.

I think you two were still in elementary school when you started to understand that others will accept or reject you based upon what you do and how you look.

As the years passed, you began to understand more and more the harsh bites of criticism.

From a very young age we all begin to learn the importance of creating and refining a public image that we believe is acceptable to others. In response, we quickly learn to keep hidden the inner thoughts and desires that might bring harsh judgment and pain.

Some people like to describe this act of creating a public persona as making *masks* to hide behind, while others like to describe it as *building walls*. I personally think the best illustration is symbolized in the construction of our own little forts. We build our fort and try to live safely within its walls—walls erected to protect us from the ridicule of our peers. The walls of the fort are intended to keep out anybody who might bring pain. During adolescence, the fort takes on an additional purpose—one that leaves many parents with the urge to do the funky monkey on a teenager's head ... but I digress.

When we are safely ensconced within our fort, and people wish to enter, we evaluate whether they are friend or foe. At the front gate of our fort, we have a ledger where we keep track of everybody's account. If our would-be visitors have a lot of positive points, we are likely to swing open the gate and invite them in. We are happy to see them, and smiles and laughter come easy. Secrets can be shared.

If the ledger indicates that people requesting entry have little or no positive balance, then we inquire through a little window in the gate to determine whether or not we want to invite them inside. Once inside, if they don't bring something that raises their balance, they are sometimes only treated with the bare minimum of courtesy. Conversations tend to be brief and sometimes uncomfortable.

If the ledger shows that people wanting in have a negative balance, they are considered a foe, and we don't let them inside. We make them holler their requests over the fortified walls. We don't want them inside. They may do or say things that hurt.

Now, the system for scoring positive and negative balances is a fickle scale. As unfair as it sounds, the reality is that attractive people are often awarded a positive opening balance. The more appealing the person, the greater the initial balance. On the other hand, if you are an unattractive person, you may start with a negative balance and have to earn your way inside.

It also isn't an accurate accounting of the pluses and minuses. The ledger's balance can change in a heartbeat. If the scorekeeper is really mad when you do something offensive, you may get a disproportionately harsh debit. If the offense tends to be a repetitive occurrence, the penalty is likely to compound. At other times you can be charged with negative points because it is merely assumed that you will say or do something bad—even if you never actually do it.

The reason the fort is the best illustration of this behavior is because it not only describes the means of your children protecting themselves from the harsh world outside, but it also illustrates how they leave you, the parent, standing on the outside while they determine whether or not you are worthy to enter. There is no better illustration of the injustice of the accounting system used when all of a sudden your sweet, open and loving little child is now brazenly expecting you to be contented standing outside the fortress walls hollering your requests from a distance.

It goes down something like this:

A dad addresses his daughter with the intention of asking her to clean her room. The daughter doesn't even have to check the ledger; nobody over 21 has a positive balance.

When dad shows up wanting in, the child instinctively knows that this could go south fast. She might have to leave the confines of her self-indulgence, so she wants him to leave his request at the gate, and she will get back to him on the matter. "What do you WANT?" she will say with only minimal courtesy.

No smiles or jovial conversation. This is business. Since it is business with somebody who has a terribly negative balance, then it couldn't possibly be a business proposition in which she has any interest. The dad knows he is standing outside the gate. He knows he is having to talk through her defenses, so he skips the formalities and gets right to the point.

"You need to do something about this room. Even the dogs are afraid to spend the night in here anymore...."

Just as she suspected! It is a hostile onslaught at the front gate. She knows from experience that dads don't like being left outside; they want in where they can talk. When she won't open the gate, he tends to want to batter the gate down. She decides to open the peephole and confront him there. "What?"

When he repeats his demands, she knows that she will have to defend her fort or spend the rest of the day doing something unpleasant. She opens the gate, but instead of letting the intruder in, she meets him outside with her sword drawn. "Why are you picking on me? I cleaned my room twice last month! You never say anything to the *Golden Child* when he doesn't clean his room. It isn't fair!"

If the dad is hard-nosed, he threatens consequences and leaves. If the dad is less hard-nosed, he tries to calm her by breaking the tension. "NASA is missing one of its space shuttles. They wanted me to check and see if it got lost in here somewhere." He is the only one who laughs at his "dad" joke, but it makes him feel better anyway, and he leaves.

The teenager, meanwhile, returns to her fort and barricades herself back inside, smug in the belief that she would never make such a ludicrous request of her own children.

The walls thus remain, until the child nears thirty —or wants a down payment for a house.

For some people, anger is one of the primary tools in their toolbox of "people handling skills." However, like dynamite, anger's usefulness is limited. Few things are made better by blowing them up.

Letting the Smoke Out

It is important that we learn from everything we see, particularly when it isn't what we expected.

One day I found myself, and various other managers, standing around a burned-out network hub—contemplating how to deal with our predicament. We had a lot of expensive computer operators who were sitting at their workstations, still drawing wages, but unable to do any work. About that time a technician walked up, surveyed the situation, and announced, "No wonder it doesn't work anymore— you let the smoke out!"

He went on to explain that when you let the smoke out of electronics, they don't work anymore. We had a good laugh at a time we really needed one, but I couldn't keep from thinking, *What would happen if this guy had kids? What kind of strange ideas would he plant in their heads?* Unfortunately (or maybe it is fortunate) this particular guy wasn't likely to ever procreate, so we will just never know....

The point is that children learn the same way adults do; we gather a little information here, a little there, and then we fill in the gaps with guesses. We glean information from what we read, hear, see, and experience. This guy's kids might well grow up believing that electronics operate on smoke.

Just being exposed to information doesn't guarantee that we will gain knowledge. Our knowledge is based upon the things we have been exposed to—and *have retained*. (I know that I was exposed to calculus and I don't remember a thing about it. Actually, I was exposed to it a couple of times because the first time I couldn't remember to do the homework.) Never mind; I digress.

When I was still young, your grandfather told me to, "Learn everything you can, while you can." It is great advice because our knowledge determines not only what we know, it also determines our outlook on life; it defines how we see things. *Narrow-minded people often see the same things as everybody else, but they choose to dismiss some information so that they can hold onto their prejudices. They see things as they want them to be, not as they are.*

Errors in our knowledge come when we have seen things we didn't understand or have misinterpreted what we saw. We can also get errors in our knowledge when we use assumptions to fill in the gaps in our understanding.

Be careful to seek truth. Seek to understand. Don't settle for poor or incomplete information, and don't let prejudice lead you to make a bad analysis of the information at hand. Strive to understand what really happened and how things really work.

Then, when somebody tells you that you just "let the smoke out" of something, you can just grin big—because you understand.

Patience and perseverance
are not a secrets you discover.
They are skills you have to hone.
Just like muscles,
they must be exercised
if they are to develop
into something beneficial.

The Tool Shed

Learning to see each other's needs was life-changing.

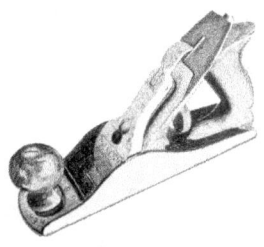

A couple of years ago, after realizing that he hadn't seen the floor of his garage in five years, our friend, Terry, concluded that he needed to build a storage shed. Eventually, Terry built a very nice shed, and his need was met. He could actually park a car in the garage again. Before he could meet that need, however, he set out on a journey that explains something we struggle with in life. The path you will travel to meet one need can actually create a lot of different and more immediate needs. Let me explain.

As he began the construction, Terry needed to dig the footers for the foundation. Because Terry's son Brett doesn't put things back where they belong, Terry's tools tend to evaporate. If you were to run into Terry while he was searching for his shovel, he would likely say that his greatest need was to find his missing tool. Was it? Not really. His greatest need was still for storage space because if he had sufficient storage space, Terry wouldn't be trying to dig holes in the backyard. At that point in time, though, he didn't see the storage shed as his greatest need. His greatest need, at that moment, was to find his shovel.

If you were to stop in a few days later, you could have found Terry once again digging through the garage. This time he would be considering military school for Brett, who he just knows was the last person to have his good hammer. Exasperated, Terry would tell you that his greatest need was for his framing hammer and possibly even a choke hold on Brett ... and at the moment he might not care in which order. Were those his greatest needs? No. His greatest need was still the storage space. That is why he was building the shed, which was why he needed the hammer.

At every new stage of the construction, things cropped up and gave Terry a new set of immediate needs. Those needs were accompanied by frustration or stress because he could not work on fulfilling his greater need until his immediate needs were first met. An observer might rightly conclude that the immediate needs were more overwhelming and emotionally charged than the greater, or ultimate need.

This happens on a personal level too. Your parents, spouse, and children will all be at different places in life and all will have their own set of needs. It can be frustrating and confusing when you step up to help someone with their immediate need—only to find that the relief you provide is short-lived and in short order is replaced by another, completely different, and yet urgent need. After this happens a few times, you begin to wonder, "Just what does it take to make this person happy?" You have stepped in to help meet the immediate need, and instead of it creating peace and contentment, it created an entirely new set of needs.

Never fear, it is a normal and natural process. The need you filled is likely to have been an immediate need, not the ultimate or greater need, so he or she will quickly transition into the next immediate need. *Our greatest needs often involve our emotional or physical well being, like the need to feel love, acceptance, or respect.*

When you buy a new house, you are attempting to fill the need for safety, status or maybe even long-term security. That house, however, will generate a lot of different and new needs ... like the tool shed. Likewise, a change in jobs brings with it a different set of needs. So does the birth of a child. What you need to take away is an awareness of the immediate needs which will be generated and the role you play in recognizing and meeting those needs.

This realization came to me when I saw your mom struggling with some simple little things—that were very much within my power to resolve—but were just not on my radar. One example was the circuit breaker that tripped every time she tried to vacuum. I could fix it in an afternoon; it was no big deal. But for her, it wasn't just an annoyance; it caused her anxiety. From my perspective, fixing that circuit was a long-term objective. I planned to eventually rewire the whole house, along with insulating the attic and updating all the plumbing. To me, those were long-term needs. I did not see the problem with that one circuit breaker as an immediate need.

She had expressed her frustration many times, but I failed to realize that, to her, the faulty circuit was preventing her from pursuing her greater need—that of caring for her family and her home. Part of her self-worth is tied to how well she cares for us, and every time she tried to clean, that circuit breaker would trip. Because I failed to take her immediate need into consideration, she experienced stress because she was having to fight with this same wiring problem every time she tried to fulfill her greater need.

At some point in time, I realized that her frustration was just like the frustration Terry experienced while trying to build his shed. I began to see her immediate needs differently, and I began to deal with them because doing so would give her some peace of mind.

I also began to notice that each of you had your hands full trying to fulfill your own needs, and that those needs were unique to you and that they were different than the collective and larger needs we had as a family. I was always pretty much preoccupied with things like making a living and the quality of your education. It just didn't dawn on me that you, too, were fighting through immediate needs, and were doing so with an intensity that rivaled any adult.

Interestingly enough, when I began to show understanding, and an interest in helping you meet your own needs, you intuitively reciprocated. It was a beautiful thing.

Learning to see each other's needs was life-changing. It was mostly an intuitive thing because we never really discussed what was happening. We just developed a willingness to look outside of ourselves when we detected a problem within each other. We began to help each other, not because we had to, but because we wanted to help deal with each other's pain.

Becoming aware of each other's needs has also helped your mom and me to be more patient with each other. We are both still trying to learn how to recognize the difference between what are just "wants" and what are "immediate needs." I also recognize that our personalities play a role. I tend to spend more energy trying to accomplish long-term objectives, and your mom tends to fixate more on the present. But just coming to that realization helped me in my struggle to get off my ass and deal with things that are causing her stress.

You can't assume that your spouse will always agree with you on which needs are most urgent. Things that give you peace of mind won't necessarily give your spouse any relief at all. Neither of you is wrong, and neither is defective. Understand that, accept it, and then give your spouse some relief by learning to pay attention to what is important to him or her.

When you have children, be respectful of their needs, and if you are as lucky as we were, they too will learn to reciprocate. I'm not saying they won't occasionally scatter your tools, and I'm not saying they won't sometimes be selfish and uncaring. Rest assured those will both occur at some point. But if your children learn to reciprocate and be sensitive to the needs of those around them, you might be spared a lot of grief. And, you will be spared hours researching military schools because no matter where you look, you just can't find your good hammer.

When you are struggling in life, the solution can usually be found in things you are just certain are not the problem....

Reality Checks Don't Bounce

The reality is that you are better off facing down the lies in your life.

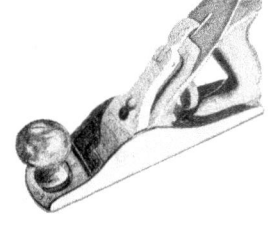

Many years ago I heard the story of a guy who bought a brand new 4-wheel drive vehicle for his commute to work. Gasoline was cheap back then so fuel efficiency wasn't yet a big priority to manufacturers or consumers. Even so, because of its really horrific gas mileage, this particular model was infamous for how much it cost to operate.

Evidently, this particular guy was not very popular with his coworkers. They viewed him as a know-it-all, a bragger, and somebody who had a very low opinion of just about everybody. According to them, this purchase wasn't about wheels for getting to and from work; it was about elevating his status and solidifying his superiority over the rest of mankind.

It is no surprise, then, that upon gathering around to inspect his brand-new purchase, his coworkers offered suggestions like adding some roof-mounted fuel tanks so he wouldn't have to stop for gas on the way to work and again on the way home. Somebody else suggested he would get better gas mileage if he just bought a wrecker and pulled it around with that. The teasing, however, had no effect. He just wasn't interested in the opinions of his knuckle-dragging coworkers.

It was on that very first day his coworkers hatched an evil plan. It was brilliant, cruel, and still managed to be funny as hell. Each day his coworkers took turns filling up a big metal gas can, and each day somebody would sneak out to the employee parking area and add the fuel to the new vehicle. The owner had no idea, however, after a few weeks, he was starting to get really smug about the gas mileage his new status symbol was getting. They kept up this little charade for nearly a month. That gave their unsuspecting coworker time to get very cocky and obnoxious about his purchase to as many people as would listen.

Of course, the day came when they stopped adding gas, and you can guess what happened. Over the weeks that followed, the guy's mood slowly went from a smug superiority to a full-blown fury. I'm certain a lot of eyes rolled at his local dealership every time this guy came in to complain about his gas mileage. The employees at the dealership had no idea what was going on. They just knew that the fuel efficiency this customer was expecting was ludicrous for this particular vehicle. Sure enough, when they put his vehicle in the shop, everything checked out just fine. That just made the guy madder. He had bought the lie, and he fully believed that he should be getting the same fuel efficiency he experienced that first month when the vehicle was brand new.

Now, you would expect that it would have raised a few red flags when he was getting twenty or thirty miles per gallon on a vehicle that is known for getting eight or nine. But, when the news is good ... who really wants to question it?

Logic should have told him that his expectations were not in line with reality. He should have suspected that something was up. But in his desire to believe he had scored big time, he bought into the lie. When the realization sunk in that he would be stuck with a vehicle that only got nine miles per gallon, he was unhappy. When he had to eat crow for arguing with everybody about the tremendous gas mileage he was getting, he was furious. He was faced with a reality check even though the realistic gas mileage had been clearly displayed on the window sticker of the vehicle when he bought it.

In those days there were lots of conspiracy theorists proclaiming that the big oil companies were conspiring with automobile manufacturers to keep the efficiency down so oil profits would remain high. As it turned out, the reality was a lot simpler, and a lot more messed up.

Of course, it was funny to his coworkers because they were all tired of his crap and they were all in on the gag. They knew the reality of the miracle gas mileage and how totally and completely their arrogant coworker had taken the bait ... and set up his own little version of reality. When something sounds too good to be true, start asking yourself, "why?" It's called *the smell test*. When something doesn't pass the smell test, it's time to stop and reassess things.

I've known people who lied to themselves for so long they completely lost touch with reality. They lived most of their life without even a hint of anything irregular, but something happened that they just couldn't deal with. They began to lie to others as well as to themselves, and it started them down a path that they didn't recover from.

Women insist they are fat when they aren't, or that they are ugly when in reality they are beautiful. Men don't think they are fat when they really are, and they believe they can get the toaster put back together, "Just like it was." *We lie to ourselves about how wonderful other people's lives are, then we fail to be thankful for the blessings in our own lives.*

We also give children labels like "slow," or "fat," or "lazy," and they will sometimes carry these lies for their entire life. Few things are more tragic than watching people live their lives without understanding how beautiful and capable they really are. But just like the coworkers adding gas to the tank, other people create the lie, and we buy into it, even when reality contradicts that lie. For some reason, it is just too easy to believe the bad stuff about ourselves and others.

When it comes to lies about ourselves, we often choose to believe the bad stuff because even though it is miserable, it is familiar, and we know we can survive. It is a comfort zone of sorts. We don't like the lies about our value as a human being, but we know we can live with that particular shame because we have done it for so long. Getting out from under the lie might expose us to larger failure, greater rejection, and an even harsher shame and that is an even more frightening prospect than the shame we carry now—so we choose the lesser of the evils and that is to believe the negatives. Our fear puts us into bondage. Negative self-talk actually reaffirms our choice. It becomes reinforcement for what we consider reality.

The reality is that you are better off identifying and facing down the lies in your life. Almost all drama, jealousy, pride, and fear are based on lies. If you have any of these in your life, confront them. Be honest with yourself about the role you played and the indulgence of living on large doses of emotion, and take responsibility for your actions and attitudes. Recognize the contribution you are making to the situation. If you lost a job or experienced a breakup that devastated you, acknowledge the role you played, own it, admit it, and accept the consequences. Our mistakes are a part of us—a part of our history—but they don't have to be our identity. Learn from them, then let them go. Move on.

Other lies that we need to fight back against are those we have been told and believed about ourselves, or about those that we love. Don't let a day go by that you don't give your children a hug and tell them that they are loved and that they are precious. Contradict the world's lie that they are anything less than a miracle. Call your spouse out when they demonstrate that they are beating themselves up because of a lie; some of which they have carried since childhood. Call yourself out when you entertain negative self-talk, which insists that you are anything less than a magnificent creature. You are beautifully and wonderfully made. Don't let anybody tell you otherwise.

If the day ever comes where you are out with friends and spy a bitter old man sitting alone at the bar, talking about a massive conspiracy between big oil and the car manufacturers ... don't bother trying to set him straight. His reality check failed to clear the bank long ago, and he won't believe a word you say.

Healthy reflection

is how we groom our soul.

It is a discipline—

and maybe even an art.

Reasonable Expectations

When things are frustrating you, stop what you are doing and evaluate your expectations.

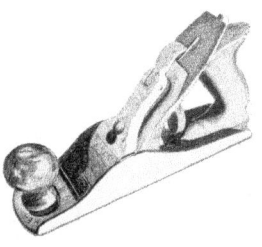

My first job out of high school, and for several years during college, I worked as a mechanic. The first shop I worked in had a guy with a nasty temper. He would get mad at something he was working on and hurl a wrench all the way across the shop. No aim, no concern for who or what the metal projectile might hit, just extreme frustration exploding. He wasn't a bad guy, but he was subject to fits of rage. His temper ruled him.

He was a great mechanic, and he was fast. He made the most money of all of us because he got things right the first time, and did so faster than anybody else in the shop. But none of us wanted to work in close proximity to him.

I experienced the same kind of anger, but I had an easier time exercising restraint. I didn't throw things, but short bouts of anger still overwhelmed me from time to time. I didn't like my anger and struggled to control it, but anger isn't something you can easily switch off. It is better fought off before it occurs.

On several occasions I had the chance to earn more elsewhere, so I packed up my tools and moved on to a different shop. When I changed shops, I remember experiencing the strangest thing. I noticed that during a repair, no matter what kind of obstacle would present itself, I was able to cheerfully overcome it, and move right on through my day. Yet, six months later, that exact obstacle would incite rage.

I also remember noticing that the "old-timers" in the shop experienced the same problems I faced, and they worked around the obstacles without any apparent emotion. To them, obstacles were just a matter-of-fact occurrence.

So ... what gives? As mechanics, obstacles cost us money. The faster we went, the more money we made. We young guys liked making money, and we liked expensive toys. To keep up the paychecks, we needed everything to go smoothly.

When I first went to work at the new shop, I was more interested in proving myself than making big paychecks. Nobody is impressed with a mechanic who is fast but does poor work, so I was more interested in showing my skill than my speed. My expectations weren't sabotaging me.

The older guys had done this so long that they had learned to set reasonable expectations, and as a result they were a bit more laid back. They made nearly as much money as we did, but they went slower. Kind of the tortoise and the hare I guess. They didn't work fast in short spurts and blow their top in between; they would keep a steady pace and stay calm. When obstacles arose that would draw the task out longer, instead of getting mad over something they couldn't control, they just adjusted their expectations and worked through the problem.

When I expected things to go at a certain speed, and then they didn't, I got frustrated. When I expected things to be simple and they weren't, I got frustrated. Getting mad didn't make things work better. Getting mad just made it more difficult for me to alter my unrealistic expectations. It felt personal. I actually felt hatred for something completely mechanical—something incapable of malice.

When things are frustrating you, stop what you are doing and evaluate your expectations. Ask yourself, "What did you think was going to happen?" *Make your expectations realistic. Regardless of what you want to have happened, reality will be dealing the cards.*

Don't let your expectations back you into a corner. When you schedule things too close together, you are increasing your chances for failure. When everything must go right in order to meet with your expectations, you are almost guaranteeing frustration.

Do the best you can to keep moving, and then adjust your expectations as the obstacles arise. Even the most sophisticated plans have contingencies for things that can go wrong. You should have them, too.

Also, guard against making your expectations self-defeating. There is a difference between anticipating possible obstacles and running around predicting failure.

Make decisions based upon
what you want your life to be
twenty years from now,
not on what you want to indulge in
at the moment.
If you live only in the moment,
your future will be
a series of events
over which you seem to have
no control.

Yeah, Right! Opposites Fight!

... your mom couldn't be more opposite. She makes Eeyore look like a motivational speaker.

Don't get me wrong ... I like my hands. They are surprisingly coordinated and strong, but they are just hands. I got the utility model. Still, they kind of define for me what hands should look like—until I see your mom's hands. We have been married for 30 years now, and I still think her hands are just beautiful. They are dainty and feminine, without being fragile. They are like a painting by one of the great masters.

I'm told the reason her hands are so appealing to me is that they are so different from my own. Opposites attract. They are just one of the many things that made me crazy about her during our teens. I couldn't get enough of her ... all of her, her mannerisms, her features, even her way of seeing things. The very things that attracted us to each other initially were our differences.

I've gone through some periods where I spent a lot of time being angry and pessimistic, but my personality always veers back toward optimism. In that, too, your mom couldn't be more opposite. She makes Eeyore look like a motivational speaker. Her favorite saying is, "Everything's futile and life sucks when you're us." She asserts that any thinking individual should be able to look around and see all the reasons why we should be depressed.

We couldn't be more different.

As the newness of marriage begins to wear off, the differences that were once wonderful are no longer celebrated. In fact, they can become an irritant and even a source of condemnation. We begin to expect that the other will "mature" or "come around" and start to do and see things the same way we do. After years of waiting, when it doesn't happen, we are tempted to conclude that the other is defective and resentment sets in.

Then, love suffers.

I could judge your mother's cynical incursions into the depths of despair as a foolish endeavor that never accomplishes anything, and she could see my optimism as evidence that her dad was right and that I am not getting smarter with age. But, she isn't a casual acquaintance. She is the person I want to spend the rest of my life with. She is my best friend. I have come to realize that she isn't defective because she doesn't see things as I see them, so I shouldn't feel the need to try to fix her. I need to love her for who she is ... the person I fell in love with.

When I accept that she is different—not defective—I am not tempted to ridicule or scold her when she is down. I make it my job to be there for her, to pick her up, to bring her back from the edge, to bring a little bit of sunshine into her life—not to criticize her for being down in the first place.

When neither of us sees the other as defective, even though we are significantly different, we can get back to the simplest kind of relationship, one without so many complications and irritations.

Even after all these years, we still choose each other. I've made the remark before, that even if we got a divorce, we would probably still live together because we truly are best friends. We would just have separate bedrooms. As bad as life might seem at times, we know it would be even worse if we had to go through life without the other. We haven't always allowed the other to be themselves, but we are getting better about it.

And, we are beginning to enjoy the differences again. We are getting beyond the age where we feel the need to change the other. We are beginning to not just accept each other as we are, we are learning to once again find the appeal in those differences.

In your adult relationships, you will sometimes experience times that you wonder, "Just what in the hell did I see in that person!" Followed shortly thereafter by, "What was I thinking!" That is a sure sign that you have allowed unrealistic—and harmful—expectations to creep in. Seeing the other as defective poisons your relationship.

When you find yourself in this position, go back and think about your love when your relationship was young. Go back and find those things that drew you together initially, those differences that you now consider defects, and reevaluate them. Think about what you celebrated about the other. Then, to find the appeal once again ... you must stop viewing the other as defective and once again appreciate the other for his or her unique characteristics. If you will celebrate each other's strengths as well as embrace the differences, you can get your relationship back.

When your mother comes barging through the front door ... complaining about the crowded stores, the price of food and the utterly useless help carrying groceries, I no longer feel the need to insist that she "count her blessings." And, for the most part, she no longer feels the need to hold up one of those beautiful little digits and proclaim, "You're lucky I've got two arms full of groceries."

If you want to know people intellectually, find out what they respect. If you want to know people emotionally, find out what they resent.

The Art of Volunteering

Nothing feels as good on your pillow as knowing that you worked hard and did the right thing.

Volunteering is as American as apple pie. America was built on people sharing their own time and talents to help each other, but it seems that volunteering is becoming a lost art.

Today, I see a lot of people who don't know how to volunteer, and when it isn't done right, volunteer help can be a real pain. When it is done right, however, the person volunteering benefits as much as, or more than, the person who receives the help. I have found few things that give me as much joy and peace as helping somebody in need.

Growing up in the country, I remember people volunteering a lot. There wasn't a lot of money to be made ranching in arid climates. People had to help each other because they couldn't afford to hire help. It just made sense to work together. It is a thrill to know that others value you enough to stop what they are doing and help you when you are in need, but that help can turn sour if it isn't done right.

First and foremost, understand that a good volunteer doesn't keep score. Some of the elderly people and widows in our community could not possibly return the amount of help they received, but that didn't matter. When they had a windmill fill with sand, or corrals that were falling down, somebody showed up and took care of it. The compensation was sometimes nothing more than a cup of coffee, and a heartfelt "thank you," although, if you worked through a mealtime, you usually got fed. You felt the real reward though when you lay down to sleep that night. Nothing feels as good on your pillow as knowing that you worked hard and did the right thing.

By volunteering, we also learned the importance of being candid. When we didn't know for certain what we were doing, we said so. We didn't want to screw things up; that would be no help to anybody. We were honest about our limitations, but we didn't use them as an excuse to get out of the unpleasant jobs.

And when it comes to unpleasant jobs, don't pick and choose what you want to do. When you volunteer to help, do whatever needs to be done—even when it is unpleasant. If you are there to help, then help; don't hinder. It all has to get done, and somebody has to do it; it might as well be you. If you are working with others, pick the most undesirable tasks, so that they don't have to do them. It may seem a bit counterintuitive, but it gives you a feeling of fulfillment you can't get any other way.

Don't be a prima donna. Show up on time. Don't expect the recipient to jump through a bunch of hoops for you. When you volunteer, you become the servant, not the other way around. Don't insist that things be done "your way." When you help people out, it is their job. They are the boss. You can put in your two cents, then shut up and do it however they want it done.

Also, be careful to work to the level of detail desired by the recipients. Don't obsess over details that don't matter to the recipients, but also make sure you don't shortchange them. Just because you are not being paid is no excuse for poor workmanship.

Most importantly, don't remind people of how you have helped them. If you keep bringing up your previous contributions, people may feel indebted or guilty instead of feeling valued. Give the gift of a job well done, and then let it go; forget about it.

I truly hope that you experience the joy of helping others as you go through life. I encourage you to volunteer not only your time, but your talents and money, too. It is a great way to give something back. But remember, volunteering is only a thing of beauty when you do it right.

Wisdom can

usually be found

hanging around

with simplicity

and tranquility.

I Can Live with That

While I missed the emotional aspects of that day, I now realize that the recognition that I had died was a defining event in my life. I was never the same.

During the couple of years that my dad drilled water wells for a living, he had a garage in town that housed the drilling tools and a couple of the work trucks, along with a little office in one corner where my mom answered the phone and kept the books. After school was out, my brother and I would walk the few blocks from the school to the garage to hang out until they closed up shop.

Because drilling wells is muddy work, the concrete floor of that garage was constantly getting large deposits of mud that hitchhiked in under the fender wells and chassis of the trucks.

I didn't do well with boredom, so even though I was only eight or nine years old, one day after school I decided to shovel out the dry clumps of mud and sweep the shop. Even after all these years, I remember my dad's reaction when he got in at the end of the day and noticed the clean shop floor. That's when he offered me my first job. He told me that if I would keep the shop swept up, he would make me an employee and pay me a dollar every week.

That doesn't sound like much money now, but back then you could still buy penny candy, so a whole dollar was a small fortune. A Sweet Tart® the size of a bar of soap cost only a dime, so I could buy a couple of those each week and lick on them until my tongue was absolutely raw. I was the envy of the neighborhood. I got a real paycheck. My mom always made a really big deal out of cutting me a check right along with all the other employees, and then she would take me to the bank so I could cash it.

From that and similar experiences, I learned that working and taking initiative was the way to get what I wanted. The positive reinforcement I got from my parents and others cultivated in me a work ethic that was a bit unusual for my age. Kids who were raised helping their parents in business or on a farm or ranch know what I'm talking about. Many of them learned at a young age the fulfillment that came from hard work.

That may be why I always loved working with my dad. I loved the feeling of acceptance and accomplishment that went with working alongside the adults and doing a good job. My dad didn't believe in being pals with his kids, so our relationship was very much on adult terms, but that was just fine with me.

Work was a chance to prove myself, and a chance to learn new things. Over my lifetime my dad had to do a wide variety of things to provide for us, and he was good at seemingly everything he touched. One week we would be building forms and pouring concrete, the next we might be doing electric or plumbing. He could overhaul an engine, weld a bridge from scratch, or dig a trench with a backhoe. He came by it honestly. My grandfather was like that, too. I came from a family of very industrious, innovative, and hard-working people.

I admired my dad's skill, and I craved his attention. He was a very patient teacher who was at his best when passing on the craftsmanship, knowledge, and the thirst for understanding that he had attained. He believed in hands-on learning, hard work, and tough love. He was a bit stingy with praise, but I could usually tell when he was pleased. And, on rare occasions, I got a glimpse of the fact that he was proud of me. I lived for those moments. My dad loved my brother as well, but there was no disputing that my dad and I were exceptionally close. We had a unique and special relationship. I preferred working with him over hanging out with friends. It's just the way it was.

One Sunday after church, I talked my dad into letting me ride to our house with AJ, an elderly rancher that my family absolutely adored. He had accepted an invitation for lunch, and I wanted to ride with him for the nine-mile trip up the winding canyon road that took us to our place. Dad was manager of a summer camp at the time, and we lived right on the property. The camp was our home.

As we arrived we drove past the house and headed for the dining hall where my mom was busy preparing lunch for the weekend guests at the camp. As the two vehicles drove through the large entryway, my dad noticed in his rearview mirror that AJ's car didn't quite make the turn. He watched helplessly as AJ's car, with me in it, hopped the sidewalk and lumbered off across the lawn. The car then lurched to a stop as the front wheels dropped over a retaining wall. His first thought was that maybe AJ was suffering a heart attack.

Dad and my brother stopped their pickup truck in the middle of the road and ran back to where the car had come to rest. They went straight to AJ's door to try and help him out. The old rancher was barely conscious. AJ was resisting their efforts to get him out of the car, though, and was trying his best to tell them something. His words were not coherent; he was in bad shape. What he was trying frantically to convey was that he was worried about me. He knew something was very wrong.

A handful of onlookers had begun to gather. It wasn't until after AJ was out of the car that somebody discovered me slumped into the floorboard on the passenger side. When they pulled me from the car, I wasn't breathing. There was no way for them to know how long I had been that way.

My dad later told me that he felt like he had the breath sucked out of him when he first came around the car and saw me colorless and lifeless on the ground. I know it had to be the hardest thing he had ever done to push back panic and despair he was feeling as he kneeled over his lifeless child, praying and listening for a heartbeat. I hope I never have to know the horror parents must feel when they realize that a child they love dearly is suddenly gone. He once claimed that time momentarily stopped as it occurred to him that this was real; it was actually happening. At age 14, I was gone without even a chance to say goodbye. There wasn't a chance to tell me he loved me, or how proud he was of me. Surely this is every parent's worst fear.

He would have been all but blinded by tears, but in situations like this, Dad could focus intently. He did not succumb to the convulsions caused by his emotions, and he didn't let them render him helpless. He knew that after the heart stops, the clock is ticking and chances for resuscitating a victim drop off sharply for every minute that goes by.

He began to administer CPR.

With every passing minute, the onset of fatigue and the lack of any response brought increasing levels of horror. They say that at some point, exhausted, he sank back onto the grass, and pulled me up onto his lap and just held me. He instructed my brother to go and get my mom. Dad said that he remembered looking up in the sky and thought to himself, "Lord, I gave him to you a long time ago. He's yours." He then pulled me up tight to his chest, and he cried.

But then he regathered his strength and resumed breathing and CPR. He was still working to resuscitate me when my mom arrived. When she saw the crowd, she knew it was serious. When she saw the despair beginning to show on my dad's face, she realized it was the moment a mother fears most.

As she fell to the ground next to me, though, she says she was startled by a horrible sound—a grotesque guttural noise from deep within my throat. It was something like a deep gag or gurgling sound. But as repulsive as it was, she said it was a beautiful thing because I resumed breathing. I didn't regain consciousness but I was alive.

It was hours before I was conscious and aware of my surroundings. I was in a hospital bed, under an oxygen tent. My chest was on fire, and I had a horrendous headache. I had no idea what had transpired. They told me that the car I was riding in had a faulty muffler and as a result, I had been asphyxiated. I didn't know what that meant, and I didn't care. I just wanted the pounding in my head to stop.

Despite my condition, I picked up very quickly on the fact that something significant had happened. The relief everyone was expressing seemed excessive, and they all had the red eyes, swollen nose and puffy faces that go with crying intensely. Whatever had happened had been an extremely traumatic experience for them. It didn't occur to me that I could have been anything more than unconscious, so it was a rather unemotional event for me. I don't remember if it was later that night or sometime the next day that they told me that I had died and been resuscitated. Whenever it was, they didn't elaborate.

It was several years before I learned many of the details. I knew better than to make my parents relive it.

Most of what I found out came from people who witnessed the whole thing. It was a long time before I heard my mom or dad discuss details, and even then, it was obvious that it remained a heart-wrenching memory.

While I missed the emotional aspects of that day, I now realize that the recognition that I had died was a defining event in my life. I was never the same. I had always been more serious than most kids, but this intensified it. As a teenager, I was trying to deal with my own mortality in a way that doesn't usually begin to hound a person before the onset of old age. Before I had attended my first prom, I was facing all the fears that bring on a midlife crisis.

I was actually an optimistic person, so I wasn't fatalistic and didn't wander around with a little dark cloud hanging over me. Deep inside, however, I worried that I was squandering my time. When most children are worrying about being cool and popular, I was preoccupied with making my mark in this world and worrying if I was making good use of my time on this earth. I wondered whether my great-grandchildren would even know my name. I was worried about how fragile life is; so much so, that by sixteen, I was back in the hospital with ulcers that wouldn't stop bleeding. Once again, a nearly fatal condition, and once again, the fragile nature of my mortality demanded my attention.

I never really talked about what I was thinking. I just assumed that everybody dealt with the same thoughts. To me, that was just life. Looking back, I can see that it accelerated the aging process. The things that motivated others my age seemed shallow and futile. The kids in my school treated me well enough, but I didn't particularly fit in. By the time I was seventeen I was longing for a wife, a house, and children.

Some of the staff and administration at my school became downright antagonistic. I was already experiencing a full-blown midlife crisis ... so the things that should have been important, just weren't anymore. I found myself unmotivated by their vision for my future. I wasn't buying what they were selling. Not able to recognize what was going on inside my head, they concluded that I had merely copped a bad attitude and was throwing my life away. In their own way, I guess they were trying to do what they thought was best for me, but, their pushing and ridicule only made me miserable. Once I graduated from high school, I didn't go back. It was nearly 40 years before I returned.

I have always craved the opportunity to try new things and explore the world around me, and I also spent a lot of time reflecting. I still do. Having all of this going through my head at such a young age resulted in me having more in common with people who were much older. Even in college, many of my friends were old enough to be my parents.

It only seems appropriate that I would either live a life full of risk—or extreme caution. I have gone back and forth between the two. But one thing is for certain; I no longer fear death. Been there, done that, and it doesn't frighten me.

After all these years, though, I have come to realize that I still have some crippling fears. First and foremost, I fear the day when I can no longer tell you and your mom that I love you and that I am proud of you. So let that be understood. I love you two more than you can imagine, even when our relationships are sometimes strained.

I used to fear being forgotten. Part of the solution to that is in this writing. While most people don't even know the first names of their great-grandparents, because of these letters, your descendants may know who I was; that I lived. My life and story, as well as the stories of those I have loved, will not be lost. I haven't chosen to focus on the stories that are most exciting to tell, or which make me look good, but rather I have focused on the stories that teach you what I yearn for you to know: To give you the best chance of living lives of contentment, success, and love. I also want you to know the story of my joys, my loves, and the perspectives that helped me find gratitude, and ultimately fulfillment, in my life.

My story is the thrill of finding and marrying your mom, and the wonder of your births. My story is the joy of watching you both discover your world, finding the love of your life, and eventually having your own children. That is what has made my whole life worthwhile. It is the real story of me.

I can live with that.

You can't fix people
who are hurting...
about the best you can do
is love them
while they cope.

Acknowledgments

I would like to acknowledge the contributions of my wife, Belinda, who has always believed that—deep inside—I possess an abundance of redeeming qualities, and she is confident that she will someday find one.

My son, Brandon, who shares my fascination for taking things apart, and my daughter Dacia, who is ever surprised that I can tie my own shoes.

I would like to acknowledge the role played by both my parents, who, to this day, swear they raised me right.

I would also like to acknowledge contributions by:

Judith Briles, my editor-in-chief, book shepherd, and champion, whose experience and wisdom have been invaluable in the process of making this series of books a reality.

Angela Thompson, my copy editor. A real sweetheart, who just loved the letters and whose patience and persistence were a critical first step in this publishing process. Angela taught me a lot about grammar.

Amanda Sorenson, my content editor, who invested long hours helping me with the content and flow of the letters. She helped me rebuild some of the heavily abridged letters so the stories once again made sense and the message came through. Amanda explained a lot to me about flow and readability.

John Maling, for his insights and help with everything from clarification and perspective, to grammar.

Rebecca Finkel, my book designer, who did a magnificent job on the design for the cover and the layout of the book's interior. Her patience and encouragement were amazing considering the number of changes she had to make before this book was ready for publication.

Ruthie Lane, a loyal friend and accountability partner, who is one of the few people who can motivate me to sit down and to write.

Kelly Johnson, everybody's favorite Geek Girl, for helping this old dog learn new tricks … at least as my computer goes. Her knowledge and encouragement continue to help me get things done in the marketing and publicity phases of publication.

Mara Purl for helping me find the heart of my stories to aide with messaging and marketing.

And for all the friends and family over the years who read the letters and encouraged me to get them published, I can't thank you enough. There are too many to list here, but I appreciate every one of you.

Turn the page for a sneak peek of
Volume II

What's Not to Trust?

Things I Want My Children to Know

Anthony Arvin
Volume II of the award-winning series

What's Not to Trust?

It became apparent that anybody who spent significant time around Bucky learned to just love him. They loved his quirkiness, his ornery streak, even his permanent bed-hair. All their affection, however, was based upon his one redeeming quality ...

Nobody ever really owned Bucky. When he changed hands, it was just the next person's turn to feed him. Bucky was a burro, and upon reflection, each subsequent owner probably only sold him because they thought it unseemly to shoot the old boy.

I was six or seven years old when it became our turn. My dad had a job working for an outfitter. As outfitters, it was their job to take customers to the best locations for hunting trophy game. Dad and a small crew of ranch hands provided food, transportation, and shelter for their customers. Before the season started, the outfitters would send their guys high into the mountains to set up a large base camp that they utilized all season long. The average hunt only lasted about ten days, but all of the various hunting seasons encompassed several months, so they built one camp and just rotated hunters and fishermen through it.

Each trip out of the high country involved taking a batch of hunters, along with their newly acquired big game trophies, back to civilization. Each trip back up to the base camp meant taking a whole new group, their possessions, and all of the food necessary for another ten days of hunting and fishing high in Colorado's Rocky Mountains. Because motorized vehicles were forbidden in the wilderness, horses were utilized for transportation of both people and goods.

It was during this period of his life that my dad ended up with Bucky.

The former owner, an elderly Ute gentleman, was quite adamant about two things. The first: he insisted the burro was only good for children to ride. The second: he caution that no matter how tempting it was, you could never, ever, trust this burro. Trust him? With what? What's not to trust? The old gentleman wouldn't go into any detail ... he just repeated himself. Never turn your back on him. Never turn your back.... Hearing this should have raised a red flag or two. Plus, it was not a common practice in cowboy country for a man to take a burro home for his children to ride. Then, the old man shuffled off with a quickened pace, cash in hand, and a smile on his face ... as if he had just done a good deed—or something along those lines.

Now, it is also important to note that Bucky was a burro, not a donkey. Despite what the occasional know-it-all will tell you, there is a difference.

Donkeys are those docile and graceful little animals featured in paintings contained in old Bibles. They are loyal, humble, and hardworking. Donkeys are affectionate and lovable. Burros are different. They more closely resemble that disquieting friend from college who only shows up in the middle of the night wanting to borrow money or to crash on your couch. Burros never have a good hair day. Bucky had permanent bed-hair, and a tendency to sneak off—no doubt—to sleep off a hangover or to lay low so the bookies couldn't find him.

Upon first sight, Dad might have been tempted to feel sorry for Bucky had he not failed to heed the old man's advice and forgotten the whole thing about turning his back. Bucky had a nasty bite and a morbid sense of humor. As is common with burros though, he did have a laid-back demeanor, so—at some point—my dad concluded that Bucky would be perfect for his string of pack animals. After all, burros are supposed to be ideal pack animals. Right? And, to be honest, Bucky wasn't all that great for us kids to ride.

The other pack animals were horses. The owner of the outfitting company had some magnificent horses, and the pack string was no exception. The upside was that the packhorses were *quarter horses,* which meant that they were strong and agile, and they could go all day carrying unimaginable loads over brutal terrain. The downside was that they were *quarter horses,* which meant that they tended to be excitable.

It wasn't all that unusual for one of the packhorses to notice a squirrel dart across the trail and respond by hosting a yard sale. Not only would the animal spread all of his goods out on the grass for everyone to see, he would then do his best to convince the other packhorses in the string to contribute their unwanted goods among the rocks, on the trees and in the streambed along about a quarter-mile stretch of the trail. Needless to say, having a calm, levelheaded and stable burro tagging along should be no bother at all. Right?

Before long, the day came for Bucky's first trip with Dad into the high country. Sometime during the hustle of getting the hunters, their horses, and the three separate strings of pack animals ready to head into the wilderness, Bucky was fitted with his own little packsaddle and his own panniers. Since burros are surefooted and calm, he was designated as the animal best suited to carry the most delicate freight of all—the eggs. The panniers on his burro-sized packsaddle were filled with dozens and dozens of farm-fresh eggs.

On this day, the convoy began to stretch out along the trail as one of the ranch hands led the hunters up the trail first, followed shortly after that by one of the three strings of pack animals. Next up came the group with the rest of the hired help, followed by yet another string of pack animals. Dad would follow the entire entourage while leading the last string of pack animals himself. The very last animal in his pack string would be Bucky. By the time it was Bucky's turn to join the parade, the hunters were well out of sight and probably even out of ear-shot through the heavily wooded forest.

That is when it happened, and several of those aforementioned assumptions reared their ugly heads. You see, when it became Bucky's turn to start up the trail, the lead rope pulled taut, and the whole "for your kids to ride" thing came into sharp focus. Bucky was a boat-anchor. All four legs were locked stiff, and he wasn't going anywhere.

When shouts, slaps on the ass (forgive the pun) and hat waving failed to release the emergency brake, it was decided to overwhelm him with a little encouragement from the packhorses to which he was tied. A quick swat on the rump of the horses in front of him resulted in the burro getting dragged along like a sawhorse, leaving four little ruts in the dust.

Over the next fifteen to twenty minutes, more and more effort was made to get the final string of pack animals going for the 20-mile trip into the wilderness. It would be hard enough getting to camp before dark and traveling these trails after dark could be lethal. This delay wasn't helping anybody's blood pressure. I wasn't there, but I can imagine that there were a fair number of colorful phrases and, most certainly, even a buggy whip employed—all to no avail. Finally, exasperated and thoroughly angered, Dad untied Bucky's lead rope from the other horses, threw the rope up over the burro's little pack saddle, and then left without him. Bucky would be riding home in a horse trailer with the remaining ranch hands.

Far behind schedule, Dad hurriedly started up the trail with the final string of packhorses. Through the trees he could hear angry shouts from the ranch hands left behind. While he couldn't hear what they were saying, he figured that they were yet to have gained the cooperation of the burro, thus having considerable trouble getting the burro into the horse trailer for the trip back down the mountain.

After several hours of steadily traveling and many miles up the trail, Dad and his string of pack animals finally caught up to the rest of the hunting party. These hunters were not accustomed to spending entire days riding on a saddle, so the outfitters would take occasional breaks to keep their customers from developing saddle sores.

As my dad dismounted from his horse, he looked back at the string of horses he was leading, and to his complete surprise, there at the end of the pack string stood that stupid burro. Bucky had escaped the ranch hands and taken off up the trail anyway, eggs and all. He caught up to the horses and just dutifully followed along. It is interesting to note that this animal had just endured considerable verbal, mental, and likely even physical abuse ... all to protest being told what to do ... only to gleefully cooperate once it was no longer what anybody wanted.

Bucky would follow you anywhere, but he refused to be led.

With time, Bucky proved to be the stuff of legend. Cowboys would talk about him around the campfire for many years after he was gone. They recalled his insufferable quirks and incredible savvy, followed by excited gestures and whoops of laughter as cowboy after cowboy showed where they had been bitten when they had gotten fond of the little beast and forgot about turning their back on him.

One of my favorite stories about Bucky was the discovery that Bucky, all by himself, could be sent 15 to 20 miles out of the wilderness to retrieve more supplies. They would rig him up with his empty packsaddle, give him a swift slap on the rump, and off he would go for the daylong trip back to the trailhead. When he arrived, Bucky would wait patiently until the pickup truck got there with his cargo. Then, once loaded, another slap on the rump would send him meandering back up the trail. He would travel all night, and the next morning he would be found dutifully standing in front of the cook tent, waiting to be unloaded. Dad claimed that Bucky never so much as broke an egg.

Another one of my favorite stories about Bucky was how he saved my dad from being lost deep in the wilderness. I am hesitant to assign any degree of nobility to Bucky's actions, and I rather suspect that he just didn't want to be bothered by the detour. However, as it happened, the two of them had tried making the roundtrip in one day, and it was way after dark before they made it back to camp. The trip, however, wasn't uneventful. At one point on the trail, navigating only by moonlight, Bucky came to a stop and just refused to follow. Dad returned for the little beast, and after what surely sounded like an episode of "marriage counseling gone wrong," Dad discovered that he had missed a turn on the trail. Bucky knew that they would be going the wrong direction, so he refused to follow. If it were not for Bucky, Dad would have gone down the wrong trail in the middle of the night, and ended up lost, deep in the wilderness.

While you begin to see that Bucky actually was an incredible animal, it is important to remember that just about the time you began to develop an affection for the little fellow, he would sneak up behind you and give you a nasty bite, for no apparent reason whatsoever.

Eventually, it became apparent that everybody who spent much time around Bucky just loved him. They loved his quirkiness, his ornery streak, even his permanent bed-hair. All their affection, however, was based upon his one redeeming quality: Bucky was rock-solid dependable. You could count on Bucky 100 percent.

Yes, you had to understand Bucky's quirks and be willing to work around them but doing so was rewarded by having one less thing to worry about, because you could depend on him completely.

In that regard, I can't keep from hoping that I have a little of Bucky in me. I know I have my barbs, and I certainly don't mind digging in my heels and saying, "Oh Hell No!" Anybody who has known me for long knows that I definitely have the "ass" part mastered. But, what I really hope to be is rock-solid dependable. I think that is a quality which is sorely missing these days. I hope we would all want to strive for that.

I really want to be the person you don't have to worry about to carry my part of the load, however insignificant that portion may be. Bucky's contribution to the overall hunting experience was rather insignificant, yet despite the magnificence of the horses in the outfit, Bucky is the animal that people remembered and grew fond of. He was the one they talked about around the campfire, and the one being immortalized in this story.

He just carried the eggs. Otherwise, he pretty much just minded his own business. Unless, of course, you forgot and turned your back on him.

About the Author

Anthony Arvin was born in the American West at a time when most people had never flown in an airplane and radios still had vacuum tubes. A whopping 10 pound baby, the author was born a month late, a revelation not lost on this publisher who has deemed this to be a permanent condition.

Anthony Arvin peaked early in life by graduating from high school, much to the delight and surprise of everyone in the one-room schoolhouse he called "The Big House."

Overcoming the exceedingly low expectations of others, he managed to find work in a variety of industries all over the world. The author bills himself as a well-traveled bumpkin. Depending upon who you ask, you could tack on the titles of master craftsman, world-class artist, writer, inventor ... and shameless liar.

A child in the sixties, he came of age in the seventies and married his teenage sweetheart. His writing reveals the strange and wonderful perspectives that can only come through a lifetime of questionable choices, shaky judgment and years of working with toxic vapors in poorly ventilated spaces.

He writes about the amazing journey of life and his fascination with the notion of growing up someday.

We're not holding our breath on that one.

A Note from the Publisher

One essential "must" for book authors today is to gather book reviews. Anthony Arvin would be honored if you would add yours to Amazon and Goodreads.

If you enjoyed *Worth a Thousand Words,* please recommend it to others. In book publishing, your enthusiastic endorsement is the best of all marketing.

At Cool Peaks Publishing, we love all booksellers, but your local independent bookstores are the heart and soul of the book industry. Drop in to see what's new and take home something you will enjoy.

A limited number of autographed copies are available from the author at *AnthonyArvin.com.* Visit Anthony's site and see what the author is up to now, explore the web pages for further insights and stories, and join in the conversation!

Working with the Author

You can reach Anthony Arvin through Cool Peaks Publishing at *CoolPeaksPublishing.com* or through his author website at *AnthonyArvin.com* where you can also see photos, read the author's latest thoughts, and connect with other readers.

∼

Anthony is a delightful speaker and loves speaking to groups, especially those intrigued with the prospect of writing their own letters and stories to their children and grandchildren. For availability and rates visit *AnthonyArvin.com*.

∼

Discounts are available for quantity purchases. For book clubs, civic organizations and those seeking volume discounts, please visit *CoolPeaksPublishing.com* for special arrangements.

∼

Media may reach the author directly by going to *AnthonyArvin.com* and visiting the media section of the website.

If you enjoyed **Worth a Thousand Words** and would like to be notified as new volumes are released, go to *CoolPeaksPublishing.com* and sign up for notifications.